REAL WORLD 101

HOW TO FIND A JOB, GET AHEAD, DO IT NOW, AND LOVE IT!

James Calano and Jeff Salzman

WARNER BOOKS

A Warner Communications Company

Warner Books Edition

Copyright © 1982, 1984 by James Calano and Jeff Salzman

This Warner Books edition is published by arrangement with
New View Press, 5370 Manhattan Circle, Suite 202, Boulder,
Colorado 80303

Warner Books, Inc., 666 Fifth Avenue, New York, NY 10103

W A Warner Communications Company

Printed in the United States of America

First Warner Books Printing: October, 1984

10 9 8 7 6 5 4

Library of Congress Cataloging in Publication Data

Calano, James.
    Real world 101.

    Bibliography: p.
    1. Job hunting. 2. Success in business. 3. College
graduates—Employment. 4. Professions. I. Salzman,
Jeff. II. Title. III. Title: What college never taught
you about career success. IV. Title: Real world one
hundred one.
HF5382.7.C34   1984   650.1'4   83-26107
ISBN 0-446-38395-3 (U.S.A.) (pbk.)
        0-446-38396-1 (Canada) (pbk.)

Typography: Ana Clair Hopperstad
Authors' Photo: Stephen Collector
Type: Century Schoolbook

REAL WORLD 101

*To Joseph E. Salzman and Gerard I. Nierenberg,
who introduced us to the Real World.*

REAL WORLD 101

Contents

Thanks to our friends, associates and heroes who have inspired and/or supported our careers, and therefore made this book possible: Bunny and Moe Belanger, David Bowen, Patti Breitman, Lori Bright, Bob Byrd, Gordon Calano, Devon Christensen, DeLynn Copley, Brian Craven, Loretta Dienst, Daniel Dienst, Bill Falkson, Ruthie Garcia, Marybeth Goodfellow, Teresa Goodwin, Robert Grimm, Caroline Gromosaik, Ana Hopperstad, Gina Improta, Jackie Janezic, Tim Leifield, Mark Lewis, Kent Lillie, Peder Lund, Lynn Moir, Ronnie Moore, Richard Morris, Robert Morris, Richard Mullaney, Richard Nachman, Joe Namath, Ettore Raccagni, Janet Snow Ritchie, Robin Rodgers, Marissa Roth, Rob Rutherford, Jeanne Salzman, Linda Santoro, Doug Shiff, Larry Schwimmer, Joseph Sugarman, Robert Warren Taylor, Ira Thomas, Teri Titchenal, Alvin Toffler, Thomas Vago, Annie Volz, Randy Weeks, Jerome Wilensky, Richard Zeif, and Buddy Zuckerman.

Preface

Real World 101 is a book of advice for the rookie professional.

First of all, what do we mean by professional? We mean, quite simply, everyone with a self-directed career: not just doctors and lawyers, but business-people, scientists, educators, free-lancers, journalists, engineers and artists. In other words, anyone who considers himself or herself to be a professional.

This book will teach you how to break into the professional world, how to contribute the most by getting the most out of yourself, how to work with other professionals, and some tips for handling the most tangible result of success: money.

Obviously that is a broad range for a book of 226 pages. Longer books have been written on ideas which we cover in less than a page. *Real World 101* is intended to be an overview, the single source for information on virtually everything you need to know to get in gear as a professional. We encourage you to pursue in greater depth the areas you feel are important to you, and have provided a reading list at the end of the book to help you find your next step.

Not all of the ideas contained in this book are new. Many are tried and true. Many are common sense. But many of them are, as far as we know, original. Regardless of origin all have been investigated, field-tested, and given our stamp of approval.

We had a hard time, as do all writers who are sensitive to social changes, deciding how to handle the third person singular pronoun. Should it be *he? He or she?* Half *he or she* and half *she or he? They?* Or should the problem be avoided altogether with more convoluted sentence structures? We chose *he or she.*

Another style clarification: sometimes we have used the first person plural *we* as the narrative voice ("We recommend this..." or "We believe that..."). Sometimes we have used it to speak for our generation, and sometimes for society as a whole. In the case of individual anecdotes we jumped to third person singular ("Jimmy recalls..." or "A friend of Jeff's..."). Don't let it throw you.

This is the first book for both of us. We put a lot of energy into it, and got a lot of energy out of it. We hope you will too.

Jeff Salzman   Jimmy Calano

Boulder, Colorado

1: The New World The New Us

Our generation is fascinated by the future—one reason being that like up-and-coming generations throughout history, we have a lot of it in front of us. A more important reason, however, is that we sense we may be the first generation to experience the future firsthand.

Progress is accelerative. It is estimated that human knowledge has increased as much in the last twenty years as it did in the previous three hundred years, and in the ten thousand years before that. Today things are really revved up. It's a good bet that we will soon be living in a world that is vastly different from the one for which we have prepared.

But different in what ways? It's natural, of course, to assume progress will continue to move in the direction it has been moving for the last few hundred years: toward even greater centralization, specialization and automation. This scenario usually leads to some sort of science fiction world, where people pop a pill every morning in lieu of eating, have robots to do all the work, and grow larger heads to hold all their new knowledge. The really troublesome aspect of this vision is that it is among the *best* possible results of a linear extension of past progress. Another scenario, yet more bleak, has mankind falling victim to a lethal mixture of low-level motivations and high-tech destruction, and blowing it all away.

Fortunately, progress does not march in a straight line. It is subject to drastic turns, and even reversals. For instance, the last watershed in progress, the Industrial Revolution (which introduced the concepts of centralization and specialization), totally redirected a world accustomed to tens of thousands of years of land-based self-sufficiency.

We are now facing another watershed. And just as the seventeenth century peasants' idea of progress was a stronger breed of ox, our visions of concrete cities under domes of glass may be well off the mark.

There is one thing we can count on, however, as we fight our way through the science fiction buffs, doomsdayers and nostalgia freaks in search of our futures. The new world will be our world. We are the ones who will build it, and George Orwell aside, nobody will be pulling the strings but us. Like past generations, we will see to it that the world we build incorporates our ideas, reflects our values and fulfills our needs.

And in a way that's not entirely true either, because as we are creating a new world, the world is creating a new us. It becomes impossible to sort out the causes and effects.

But that doesn't stop us from trying to sort them out. While it may be impossible to *know* the future, is is not impossible to identify and extrapolate trends. Futurism, a semiscientific discipline of social prediction, has grown up in response to our need "to know." From the judgments of futurists, and from a simple feel for which way the wind's blowing, we can put together a pretty good picture of some of what we can expect in the new world.

In the following pages we will investigate this picture. We will identify four major trends that are shaping up, and take a brief look at how they will affect our lives as professionals. And vice versa.

Trend #1: Higher Needs

If you remember anything from college, it probably includes psychologist Abraham Maslow's hierarchy of needs. If not, here's a quick refresher. Maslow theorized that people have several layers of needs. The lowest needs are physical (food, water, shelter), followed, respectively, by the needs for security, love, self-esteem, and self-actualization. Only after we have achieved fulfillment on one level are we motivated to seek fulfillment on the next higher level. For instance, when a person's physical and security needs are met, he or she may seek love. But if the lower needs are threatened, he or she will forget about love until the needs of safety, shelter and hunger are once again satisfied.

It seems that groups of people—even whole societies—function in much the same way. The needs may vary, and certainly societies operate on many levels at the same time, but the dynamic is the same. When one need is met—and only then—are we driven to fulfill the next higher one.

So how high on the need hierarchy are we as a society? There is no question that, despite pockets of deprivation, our physical needs for food, water and shelter are being well met. In fact, the biggest problem with food in our society is that we eat too much of it. Our generation, two generations removed from the Great Depression, has had more material wealth than any generation in history.

The second level of need, security, is also being met for the most part. Although many of our streets are not safe and the threat of Armageddon continues to hang over our heads, we have a fundamental expectation, justified or not, that our society is safe and stable.

The fact is, no society in history has had its basic needs so well provided for on such a large scale. As a result, an exciting transformation is beginning to take place. Our society is moving past its preoccupation with accumulating and protecting material wealth, and on to a quest for higher needs. We can see it within ourselves, in the form of a deep-seated distrust of materialism, and a new emphasis on health, personal fulfillment, psychic well-being, and other "extra-material" needs. These are fundamental changes, and our generation is at the vanguard.

Obviously this transformation will have a profound effect on the professional world, which was founded and has been based on the concept of producing wealth. It's not that we will abandon our dedication to material wealth any time soon (after all, we will continue to need the stuff). But it will be supplemented with a new emphasis on fulfillment and esteem.

More than money. Craig, a friend of J̶ successful one-person drafting shop in the basement of his home. Recently one of his clients offered to hire him full time. Craig likes the client, and the offer represented a substantial increase in income. But after thinking about it a few days, he turned it down. "Sure the job offered more money," Craig explained. "But to tell you the truth, I don't think I would be happy working for someone else. I like the freedom of having my own business. Besides, my wife and I make enough money already."

Enough money? That kind of attitude was unheard of in our parents' generation. But it is typical of our feelings, and it has old-guard personnel managers pulling their hair out. Our friend Marybeth was criticized by her boss for a lack of "soldierability" when she refused to salute and march off to a new position in Detroit. She's not unusual, though; today over half of all professionals who are offered a promotion in another city turn it down.

More and more, money is going to be less and less the central motivator of our careers. Today we need to feel that work is more than just a means of making money to buy the things we enjoy. We expect work to *be* one of the things we enjoy, and in which we can find purpose, exercise our creativity and achieve fulfillment.

Accommodation of the individual. Ironically, the shift in emphasis from production to fulfillment is still ultimately an issue of productivity: people work better and produce more when they are happy.

And when they're not? *Burnout* is one of the new buzzwords among professionals. It's the process of becoming immobilized by one's work—losing one's energy, creativity and enthusiasm. Simply put, burnout is the result of years of "putting out" energy, creativity and enthusiasm on the job without taking enough back in. And money, while important, is no substitute for these internal rewards. Studies of the American workforce consistently show that achievement, appreciation and the actual process of making a contribution are far more motivating and satisfying than money.

Yet there are millions of people—those who think they work just for money, or who work for companies who think they work just for money—who have become walking zombies. Clearly, unrestrained ambition and materialism create people who are not only unhappy, but also unproductive. As that fact has become accepted in the mainstream, things have begun to change dramatically.

The new world will have many options designed to accommodate our individual needs. We're seeing some of them now, in the form of flex-time (where workers set their own hours), increased vacation leave and sabbaticals, more part-time employment, even "mental health" days. Also, the line between labor and management will continue to blur, with employees having a significant management power, if not ownership, in their companies.

Again, the reason is simple: we are sufficiently educated and enlightened to be able to handle this kind of freedom responsibly, and too well-educated and enlightened to accept anything less.

Multiple and ad hoc careers. People under thirty-five change jobs on an average of once every year and a half. It is estimated that these young professionals will change careers three to five times in their lifetimes. For those of us who wondered how in the world we were ever going to cope with the *40/40 Rut* (forty hours a week for forty years) this is good news: we won't have to.

But isn't this kind of fluid, transitory career approach shallow, insecure and ultimately counter-productive? Not necessarily. Although our circumstances and surroundings may change with each new job, our basic needs for belonging, security and achievement will not. Fulfilling these needs in a condensed time frame will, however, demand a new consciousness—a consciousness today's young professionals have already begun to exhibit. Like professional athletes, we are becoming accustomed to changing teams abruptly, and yet playing with complete commitment on each new team. Over the course of our careers, it will not be unusual for us to form strong professional partnerships around a particular project and dissolve them with good will when the project is ended. In the new world full commitment will not necessarily mean lifetime commitment.

Job security will likewise be redefined. For instance, we will feel just as secure with a career "in the computer industry" as our fathers felt with a career "at IBM."

There is a down side to all this, too. With multiple careers we lose some of the benefits company consciousness provides. Professional training, for example, will be more of a personal responsibility in the new world. Organizations will not be inclined to invest heavily in developing people when they cannot count on reaping the returns. Likewise, they will be less inclined to stick it out with employees with whom they are having problems.

Multiple bottom lines. Higher needs in the new world apply not only to the relationships between the organization and its members, but also between the organization and society as a whole.

No longer will company executives have the luxury of making decisions exclusively on the basis of dollars and cents—not when their decision could poison a river, devastate an economy, or disrupt the lives of their employees. Nor, we trust, will they want to. Companies will operate according to what Alvin Toffler calls *multiple bottom lines*, where social and ethical issues weigh as heavily as financial ones.

Trend #2: The Specialized Generalist

Specialization is one of the "big ideas" of industrial society. The principle dictates that each person becomes an expert in one area of production, and joins together with experts in other areas to form a complete and efficient whole.

Specialization is still very much alive. In fact, as society has become more and more complex, the pressure for specialization has increased, fracturing specialties into subspecialties. Today, every professional is a specialist. We have no choice; the body of knowledge in any profession is so vast and varied that it would be impossible for anyone to be an expert—or even competent—in every area of his or her field.

Fortunately for those of us who don't want to be slid into a slot, the trend toward specialization does not continue indefinitely. Scientists have discovered that at higher levels of complexity, certain natural phenomena cannot be understood in terms of their components, but only as a whole. Likewise, many of our human systems have reached levels of complexity where continued reductionism and specialization is counterproductive. Take the assembly line for instance. The classic symbol of the power of specialization, it is today becoming a symbol of the inadequacies of specialization. Assembly line workers, having no sense of the context of their work (and therefore no sense of accomplishment and esteem), are unmotivated, even hostile. Another problem with the assembly line is the interdependence of functions; a breakdown of one component is apt to stop the whole line cold. Considering these factors—particularly the human factors—it turns out that the assembly line is less efficient than many other production approaches.

One more efficient approach is the quality circle, a Japanese concept whereby a small group of workers is responsible for seeing a manufacturing process through from beginning to end, and workers trade off their areas of specialty. That means each worker is familiar with every area of production, which fosters a sense of accomplishment and fulfillment in the final product. Not only is the worker happier and more productive, but the quality of the product is better.

As a rule, professionals have not had to deal with isolation and detachment the way assembly line workers have. But professionals do suffer from overspecialization. Some lawyers, for example, work on nothing but divorces. Computer designers sometimes spend years working exclusively on the design of one aspect of one machine. There is a real danger in this. When professionals lose sight of the overall context of their work they become chauvinistic. Obsessed with their own circumstances, they develop an us-against-them posture toward groups with which they should be cooperating.

So while the pressure to specialize has not really abated, it is being joined by a growing pressure to generalize. Fortunately, the two forces are not mutually exclusive. When we are conscious of the big picture we naturally perform better within our specialties. We don't waste time on the trivial. We see our specialties as part of a bigger result, rather than ends in themselves.

Trend #3: Higher Tech

You've heard all the incredible statistics. Computer use has grown 10,000 times since 1965. The per function cost is down by a factor of 100,000. Or to look at it another way (and this is a great image): if the automobile industry had kept up with the computer industry, a Rolls Royce would cost $2.98 and get 20,000 miles to the gallon.

What is even more incredible than the explosive advances made by the computer, is how easily—and eagerly—we as a society have adapted to it. Within fifteen years we have allowed ourselves to become computer addicts, hopelessly dependent on the blinking box for the most basic functioning of our systems: manufacturing, communication, education, research, medicine... everything.

We hear from some people that our dependence on the computer is dangerous and dehumanizing. But is it any worse than our dependence on electricity, or even the telephone? People have always been suckers for the new, the fast, and the easy. Sure, sometimes it has gotten us into trouble, but with few exceptions, the advantages of progress have far outweighed the disadvantages.

The advantages of the computer are phenomenal. It's simple: the computer does what it does far better than we ever could. In that way it is actually humanizing, because it frees us to do what we do best, like think and feel. As a whole, our society has formed a wonderfully positive and productive relationship with the computer.

And it's only just begun. A basic understanding of how to work with computers is one of the most valuable skills you can have as a professional in the new world. If you are intimidated by computers you should get over it—fast. Fortunately, computers will be glad to meet you halfway. We are currently witnessing the development of "user-friendly" computers, which enable people with virtually no special training to interact with computers using English commands. As Theodore Nelson says, "Any nitwit can understand computers; and many do."

Within the next few years we will even be able to routinely communicate with computers verbally. It is reasonable to expect that at some not-too-distant point in our careers, dealing with a computer will be no more difficult than dealing with a colleague, albeit a rather colorless colleague.

One of the most dramatic aspects of the computer revolution is the area of telecommunications. Satellite and two-way video is fundamentally changing the ways we do business. In some ways communication is beginning to supersede transportation.* It looks as though before long, many of us will be able to report to work every morning via a video terminal beside the bed. It will be common for us to work closely and directly with colleagues all over the world. These new ways of "getting around" open a world of options to us.

Further, the exciting advances in telecommunications are also likely to bring about basic changes in consciousness. Professionals will be able to work more at home rather than going to a central office every day. Changing jobs may not require moving, but rather a simple change of access codes. Ironically, it turns out that the results of high technology could very well be an enhanced sense of stability, community and family.

The change in consciousness will also take place on a global scale. Marshall McLuhan talked about the Global Village; Buckminster Fuller called it Spaceship Earth. Telecommunication will allow us to routinely interact, professionally and personally, with people all over the world. As we come to experience and appreciate firsthand our common interests as human beings, we will think and act less as citizens of a country and more as members of a global community. The resulting global consciousness will supersede nationalism on every level: production, currency, language and culture.

This change in consciousness is not necessarily a force for human homogenization. On the contrary,

---

*This single phenomenon may be the central factor in solving our energy and environmental problems.

it frees us to choose our interests from a wider range of options, and to pursue them in greater depth. It's already happening. For instance, to be a good cook in America twenty years ago generally required a facility for meat and potatoes. Today it is not uncommon for a good cook to whip up a ratatouille one night, enchiladas the second, and falafel the next.

Nor will the change necessarily foster harmony. We will still form alliances; we will just form them more according to interest rather than proximity. For example, when the American air traffic controllers walked off their jobs in 1981, the air traffic controllers in Portugal staged a slowdown in sympathy. A Portuguese controller may have felt that he or she had more in common with an air traffic controller in the United States than with an engineer down the street—and rightly so.

Trend #4: Turmoil

Obviously we are in for some heavy changes in the coming years. Unfortunately, change rarely occurs smoothly, because in order for a new world to be built, an old world, with its old vested interests, has to be dismantled.

You don't have to be a mystic to see the problems shaping up for our generation. Even today our industries, grown to monstrous proportions by a world bent on centralization, are suffocating under their own weight. Our political structures are struggling to keep up with a society far larger and more diverse than that which they were designed to govern. We are menaced by terrorist groups and states whose level of enlightenment falls far short of their capacity for destruction. Our sick economies seem to be incurable, if not undiagnosable. We are witnessing the advancement of technologies that have the power to render the planet unfit for life.

Progress itself breeds turmoil. People have a love-hate relationship with progress. We rush to embrace the new; then, when the novelty is over and nostalgia sets in for what we have left behind, we step away. Two steps forward, one step back. The net effect is forward movement—sometimes rapid movement—but it is invariably a bumpy ride.

Another intrinsic problem with progress is that the faster it moves the faster it accelerates. As those people and societies who are further ahead continue to move faster, the gap between the haves and have-nots widens. This is very dangerous, and it raises an interesting point: if indeed we are the haves (and we are), it is up to us to narrow the gap between us and the have-nots? Can we do it?

And, even more critical, can we protect ourselves in the meantime? How do people who have been enlightened to the point of regarding the use of force as distasteful and unethical protect themselves against those who use it willingly? We will have to deal with this issue on many levels, from the militaristic Soviet Union, to the high-tech terrorists, to the criminals on our streets.

Wait a minute, you say. Suddenly all this new world business is beginning to sound not-so-great.

That's because the new world is also the Real World, and in the Real World things do not always turn out for the best. Which brings us to the central issue of our generation: can we hold it together as we move it ahead? Will our consciousness keep up with our technology?

The answer, as they say, lies within. For each of the problems we are facing there are a hundred opportunities for positive action. Sure, doomsday is possible—it is frighteningly possible. And maybe it is natural to fear the future. After all, it represents the unknown which, at the very least, requires the inconvenience of adaptation. But we, like all new generations, have no choice but to reject these attitudes. We have to think we have new answers and be eager to try them out. To us the future is a challenge, and change is part of the fun.

Fortunately, we have a lot in our favor. For instance, telecommunications, as we mentioned earlier, could be the solution to our energy problems. Other emerging technologies, such as ocean farming, weather control and genetic engineering, all offer fabulous potential for progress. And to get a bit mystical for a moment, a very real possibility exists that further enlightenment could completely change the rules on this planet.

There is something each of us can contribute, and if we look around, and inside, we will see what it is. But we must make it a priority. Nothing is more important. We have more to lose—and gain—than any generation in history.

2: How We Did It

It wasn't that long ago that we were what and where you are now, newly minted professionals facing the Real World. We were, as maybe you are, apprehensive and unsure about where to go, what to do and how to do it.

Several years later, we can safely say it has turned out far better than either of us expected. Now in our mid-twenties, together we own four thriving companies doing an annual combined sales of over five million dollars, we're working with exciting people on exciting projects, and generally having a great time of it. We even wrote a book! In some ways it's been easier than we thought it would be, and in some ways much harder. At any rate, we learned a lot.

In this chapter we will share with you how we, personally, got through the precarious starting-out years. Everyone's story is different, so we offer these experiences not necessarily as blueprints for you to follow, but rather as lessons from which you, too, can learn.

Jeff

I never wanted to be a businessman. I wanted to be a doctor—a pediatrician, to be precise. That was when I was six.

Next I wanted to be a political scientist, whatever that is. I settled on political science when I was fourteen, after my older sister Jackie turned me on to *The Fountainhead* by Ayn Rand, the queen of capitalism. Those of you who know of Ms. Rand know she can be pretty potent stuff, particularly for a fourteen-year-old. I became enamored of her. I bought and read all her books (although I will now admit for the first time ever that I did skip some of the "This is John Galt" section near the end of *Atlas Shrugged*), and spent more money than I made working a whole month at Tastee-Freeze on a subscription to her monthly newsletter.

Then, as often happens to overly politicized adolescents, I became strident and obnoxious. I quoted Ayn Rand to my friends, who at that point were far more interested in the philosophy of Mick Jagger; I interrupted adults in conversation; I observed the world with an air of outraged superiority; and when I was sixteen, I was asked to leave the church my great-grandparents helped build because I was preaching agnosticism to my fellow Youth Group members.

When it came time to sign up for college, and most of my fellow recruits were wrestling with the decision of what major to declare, I still had no doubt. Political science was for me. As I think back, I can't recall exactly what I intended to do with it—become a political philosopher, I guess. Fortunately that was a reality I never had to face. In college, my life took a turn.

I went to a state-owned university in Pennsylvania called Indiana University of Pennsylvania (confusing, I know), a common choice among the college-bound of the working class in western Pennsylvania. Usually overshadowed by Pitt and Penn State, IUP is a pleasant, academically sound school of about 13,000 students located in a town of about the same size in the foothills of the Allegheny Mountains.

During my first week in college, on impulse, I joined the staff of the student newspaper. It turned out to be the first step of my first career. I was immediately assigned to write a feature article about Aquatots, a program for infants who swam in one of the university's pools. Next, I think I did something on plans for the school's new library. One thing led to the other, and before long I was promoted to positions on the newspaper where I began earning money and credits. When it came time to start thinking about graduating and getting a job, I had accumulated enough credits on the newspaper to graduate with a journalism major in addition to my political science major. This was a lucky break, because I still didn't know what a political scientist did for a living. But now I didn't care. I was a journalist.

So what does a journalist do for a living? I knew I didn't want to be a cub reporter making $12,000 a year covering city council meetings for some county daily somewhere. And I didn't think I had the experience or portfolio to get on the staff of a magazine, at least not one I would have wanted to work for. The only other option open to me, or so it appeared at the time, was advertising. (I know now that advertising is not necessarily an option open to journalism majors. There are advertising courses for that sort of thing.)

I must say I had very mixed feelings about going into advertising. On one hand, I considered it to be institutionalized lying and manipulation, a means by which people are made to buy what they don't want and want what they don't need. In fact, during my junior year I had become actively *anti*-advertising. After reading *Subliminal Seduction,* by Wilson Bryan Key, I began lecturing to various classes and groups on campus about how Madison Avenue supposedly manipulates our subconsciousness by hiding things like skulls in the ice cubes of liquor ads, and camouflaging nasty yet titillating words on *Playboy* centerfolds. Everyone was outraged. I was outraged, too.

But I was also fascinated. I was awed by the power of the jingle, slogan and slick layout. I laughed with the Volkswagen "ugly is only skin deep" campaign. I was perplexed by the intended (I hoped) stupidity of the "two housewives in a kitchen" genre. I was turned on by the sheer perfection of the models that stared out at me from magazines. I even got the old lump-in-the-throat over the packaged patriotism of the oil companies. And if it was all just a trick (and I was not convinced it was), then it was just all the more fascinating.

In the end, fascination conquered trepidation. I went into advertising.

Apprenticeship

About two months after graduating from college,

I began working as a copywriter at Wilson Reed Associates, a twenty-person advertising agency based in Youngstown, Ohio. Wilson, the president of the company, in his middle thirties at the time, had recently taken over the company from his father, who had run it for nearly forty years.

Wilson was obviously impatient with the conservative stance the company had established. And in the face of a shrinking local economy (the steel industry was dying), he pulled what I can see now was a pretty gutsy move: he expanded. A couple of months before I was brought on, the company hired three full-time artists. Plus, two other new people started the same day I did.

The fact that I was the first full-time copywriter the agency ever had, mixed with the upheaval the company was going through, created an ideal climate for me. I was stepping into an open-ended situation. My bosses didn't have much more of an idea about what I was to do than I did. I was free to create my own niche.

Who would have thought dingy old Youngstown would have offered so much opportunity? In my very first month on the job, I was writing newspaper ads for the agency's Youngstown community image campaign (a tough assignment, believe me), writing and starring in a training skit for bank tellers, and putting together a technical slide show on glazed structural facing tile.

Eventually I was assigned to supervise some of the agency's smaller accounts. It was about a year into the job, and on the eighteenth or twentieth of these small accounts, that I struck gold...in a bronze foundry. Albco Foundry was a small but prosperous bronze foundry in a small town in rural Ohio. They had contacted Wilson Reed Associates to do a company brochure. They were very clear that they wanted a first-class brochure, but they were also very clear that that was all they wanted.

To an advertising agency, the most profitable business is media advertising (because of a lucrative commission system). Projects like the Albco Foundry brochure were profitable to be sure, but considering that it was just a one-shot deal, the account wasn't terribly valuable.

"The perfect account for Jeff" seemed to be the prevailing point of view. "Challenging, full of potential, but if he screws it up, so what? The account really doesn't add up to much."

Okay by me. I was excited by the opportunity to have total control over a relatively big-budget project, and I dove in full-force. I read everything I could find on casting bronze. I taped long interviews with the company's management. I took roll after roll of photos of the plant. I went out of my way to engage the support of Bob, the agency's new art director, who agreed to work on the brochure personally.

When I look back I can see I spent far too much time on the Albco project, considering what the agency was being paid. But my bosses didn't seem to mind, and if they didn't mind, I certainly didn't. All I wanted was to produce the best brochure the agency had ever done.

And it *was* the best, at least in Bob's and my less-than-impartial opinion. More important, our bosses liked it. In fact, they decided to enter it in the Business and Professional Advertising Association's annual advertising awards competition... which turned out to be the next big event of my professional life.

Being entered in the BPAA competition is quite an honor for a rookie, and I was thrilled. Of course I didn't expect our brochure to win anything—not against the best work of the biggest and best advertising agencies in the region (including Cleveland and Pittsburgh, the big cities). Or did I? Admittedly, I may have had a couple David and Goliath fantasies about walking off with something, but I refused to allow myself to entertain any real hopes. Bob, who had been in the business a lot longer than I, said he thought we might have a chance for an honorable mention... but I think I detected some guarded hope for something better on his part, too.

As the day of the awards banquet approached, it was more and more on my mind. On the night of the banquet, as I walked into that huge hotel ballroom, I was wired. Throughout dinner it was all I could do to make small talk and eat a few bites. I couldn't get my fantasies out of my mind. I kept looking at the podium on the stage imagining myself accepting my award..."First place, full-color brochure goes to Wilson Reed Associates, Albco Foundry...Jeff Salzman, Account Executive," the master-of-ceremonies would announce. "Who's that?" everyone would murmur, as I strode to the front of the ballroom. "Why, he's just a kid..."

Reality invaded my fantasy when the awards presentation commenced. I sat anxiously as the program moved through all the various categories: newspaper ad... magazine ad, single color... magazine ad, full color... direct mail package... series of three or more direct mail packages...corporate brochure, single color...

And finally our category: corporate brochure, full color. The first award was to be honorable mention. Bob and I exchanged glances. The master of ceremonies opened the envelope, and read "Honorable mention goes to..." someone I had never heard of. What a relief. I'd rather get no mention than honorable mention, I thought. Who wants to be recognized for being less than the best?

Second prize was the same story. We didn't get it, and ultimately, I didn't care. What I wanted was coming up next. I could hardly sit still.

Now the master of ceremonies was slowing down. The first-place award in our category was one of the night's biggest awards, and it warranted a little drama. He opened the envelope and smiled at the audience as he slowly unfolded the card. He cleared his voice. "First place for full-color corporate brochure goes to..."

I couldn't help myself. I was wild with excitement. It *is* me...

"Ammons & Mauney, for United States Steel, Stainless Tubing Division."

I looked at Bob and he looked at me. It was over. We hadn't won against all odds. To hell with it, I'm glad it's over, I thought. So what if I didn't win anything—at least now I could forget about it and get back to work.

That was a bitter lesson for me, but I had earned it. Things had been coming pretty easily so far. I had gotten to be far too cocky far too quickly, and a good, solid jolt of reality was just what I needed. It's simple: in the Real World the first-year rookie doesn't single-handedly beat the veterans. And in the Real

World, they don't give advertising awards for a brochure on a bronze foundry nobody has ever heard of. It was one of the most valuable lessons I could possibly have learned at that point in my career.

It was an even more valuable lesson to unlearn. Suddenly everyone at the table was looking at me. Something was happening. I looked up at the master of ceremonies and he was looking at me too. Then through the fog of my disappointment and introspection it became clear why we hadn't won anything in our category.

We had won the best in *all* categories: the *Best of Show!*

I was stunned. I was confused. And at the same time I knew exactly what was happening...the heavens were opening up and blessing me. I was charmed. To hell with lessons in patience and humility—I was the hottest shit to hit these parts in years.

Within two weeks after the awards banquet, my salary had nearly doubled. The first phase of the increase came the day Wilson walked into my office and said he had decided to increase my salary $200 a month. That was a big raise to get in one shot, but I was confident I deserved it, and happy he thought so, too.

The plot was to thicken. The same afternoon I received a call from Baxter & Arnold, a fairly well-known advertising agency in Pittsburgh. They wanted to talk about the possibility of me coming to work for them. "No harm in talking," I said coolly, "people do it every day." (I didn't really say that, of course. But the call did bring on another arrogance attack, and if I didn't say it, I'm sure I thought it.)

I had no intention of working for Baxter & Arnold. For one thing, I was loyal to Wilson Reed Associates—it was a good agency with good people who had given me every chance in the world. Another reason—by far the stronger one—was that I had already decided to move to Colorado in six months (more on this in a minute), and I didn't want to start a new job just to quit.

Still, I felt I owed it to myself to check out the option. Although it was only remotely conceivable that Baxter & Arnold could make me an offer I wouldn't refuse, I was still eager to talk. My primary goal was simply to find out what I was worth on the open market—an important thing to know.

The day of the meeting with Baxter & Arnold I was in great form. Since I really wanted to find out how much I could make them want me, I had prepared a super presentation. But since I really didn't want the job, I was freed of the debilitating anxiety that often accompanies job interviews.

It worked. Within our first hour together they had offered me a starting salary close to double what I was making at Wilson Reed Associates. I told them, with all the nonchalance I could muster, that I would think about it.

Think about it was all I could do for the next several days. It wasn't that I was seriously thinking about taking the job—I had made up my mind to move west. More than anything I was thinking about what was happening to me. I was moving into a new phase of my career and life. I was becoming what I had prepared twenty-two years to become: a professional. And suddenly other professionals were respecting my abilities, and offering to pay big money for the use of them. I was excited; I was apprehensive; I was sad for the ending of what I perceived to be a more carefree era of my life.

Luckily, these periodic bouts with introspection didn't keep me from functioning. I knew I wanted to take things one step further—I had to find out if Wilson thought I was worth as much as Baxter & Arnold did.

I met with Wilson and told him everything that had happened: who had offered me a job, how much they had offered, and that in the interests of my career I felt I had to consider it. I told him I would stay at his agency if he would match my other offer, otherwise I would complete the projects at hand and leave.

He didn't say yes. In fact for a few long moments he didn't say anything at all. His coop had been raided, there was mutiny brewing, and he had to regroup. Finally he said simply that he appreciated my position but he would have to think about it.

Fair enough. I couldn't blame him for wanting to think. Besides, I was pretty sure he would say yes. Which he did. The next morning as we passed each other in the hall, he grabbed me by the arm. "Okay, I'll match it," he said. "We've got a lot of work to do around here." That was all that has ever been said about it between us.

Three months later I had to tell him I was leaving for good.

There were many reasons for my decision to move to Colorado. I had visited two friends there a few months earlier, and, as they say, fell in love with the place. I knew I had to leave Youngstown, a town which, although populated by warm and wonderful people, is a rather unappealing place for a young person who thinks maybe he would like to try conquering the world.

Besides, I had worked at the agency for nearly two full years, a respectable first-time tenure. And, the job was beginning to lose its excitement. I had done pretty much all there was to do at Wilson Reed Associates—I was beginning to run the second lap.

But underneath all these good, practical, career-related reasons lay the biggest reason of all: I had wanderlust. And I had it bad.

The dreaded time when I had to tell Wilson finally came. I assured myself that I was leaving the right way, that I had given the company its money's worth, that the three months' notice I was willing to give was more than fair, that it was okay to have withheld my decision about leaving when I was engineering my big raise, and that this was the way things were done in the Real World. I believed all that (I still do), but even so I felt like a heel.

Wilson was, thank God, great. He wasn't terribly enthusiastic about my decision, but he sympathized, and supported it. We agreed I would continue to work at least another three months, or as long as it took to finish the projects I was working on, and help train a replacement. ("Just *try* and replace me," I thought. Even in my gratitude, I couldn't avoid an occasional arrogance attack.) Then I would be on my way to beautiful Boulder, Colorado.

Colorado Free-Lance

Four months later I was there, or rather here, as I am still here. It's been a good move. If someone were to ask me to describe the ideal place for me to live, I would describe a place very much like Boulder. Boulder is the perfect balance of big-city amenities, small-town character and the great outdoors. It is located in one of the most naturally beautiful places in the world...a valley so perfect you'd think it came off the drawing boards of Walt Disney Studios. In my more cynical moments, of course, I think it is too perfect. But what the heck, you can't have everything.

When I arrived in Boulder I was not looking for a professional-type job. I had some money saved, and I just wanted to cool out and relax for a while. To keep myself busy, and buffer the drain on my savings account, I took a job as a sandwich-boy (which is but one caste higher than bus-dog) at the New York Delicatessen, the place that Mork has since made famous in some circles. I enjoyed making sandwiches; it was good, hard, mindless work. Best of all, I could forget about it when I walked out of the place at night.

Soon, however, it started to get to me. The indifference I received from the customers and had so enjoyed in the beginning, suddenly began to feel like lack of respect, and I resented them for it. The people I worked with had a "do as little as possible" attitude that I found irritating. Before long, even the idea of bailing buckets of grease out of a pastrami vat and slicing the taste buds off the tongues of cows (a *very* disgusting thing) began to lose its appeal.

It was clearly time to get back to work.

My friend Tim was the general manager of a publishing company in town, and over his objections of mixing business with friendship, I coerced him into pulling the necessary strings to get me hired. Like many Boulder companies, this publishing house was fairly loose. I was hired as a sort of "odd-job" editor. In the first few months I put together a book on herbs, a junk-mail package promoting an academic journal on political violence, a brochure on solar energy, and a couple fliers...fun and open-ended projects, but ultimately low-energy. I was also not making the kind of money I was looking for.

I needed something more. Tim, too, was feeling a little stagnant, so we put our heads together to try to come up with a project that would absorb our excess creative energy—and maybe make us a buck in the process. After a couple months of on-and-off searching, we hit it: we would start a magazine. During a high-energy, many-mile, all-night walk through the deserted streets of Boulder, we worked out the details. We would call the magazine *MAP, Uncharted Terrain.* It would be a monthly tabloid consisting exclusively of full-page ads for the hundreds of boutiques, restaurants, galleries, interest groups, artists and craftspeople, theaters, musicians, and entrepreneurs for which Boulder is known ...plus each issue would feature an interview with one of Boulder's celebs.

Within a month, all systems were go. We had put together a solid, realistic business plan. The owner of the publishing company, Peder, was set up as an investor (in retrospect, *set up* probably isn't such a bad choice of words), we had office space, a printer, distributor... everything but a staff and clients.

The idea was to make each page of *MAP* a work of commercial art (how else could we expect people to read a magazine of ads?). To accomplish this, we decided to put together a cooperative of twenty-five free-lance commercial artists—illustrators, designers, writers and photographers—to both sell and produce the ads. To round up this stable of artists, we ran a classified ad in the newspaper. Boulder, as you may have heard, is crawling with artsy types, and by the time the ad had run just one week we had almost two hundred responses.

Rather than explain the concept of the magazine to each artist individually, we scheduled a mass meeting where we could talk to all of them at once. Those who were interested could then sign up for an individual interview.

The night of the meeting came and so did the artists, nearly all two hundred of them, eager to find out what kind of future our new magazine held for them. We, too, were eager. I had been preparing my talk all week, shooting slides and putting them in order, organizing my points and memorizing clever twists of phrase. Tim, Mr. Public Relations, had spent the entire day organizing the meeting room, checking the details, and buying expensive imported beer.

The meeting went splendidly. Everyone got pleasantly drunk, the slide projector worked, I remembered all my twists of phrase, and Tim was at his slick, personable best. Everyone thought the magazine was a terrific idea. It turned out to be one of those magical evenings when, even in a large group, everyone's energy mingles and things happen.

The concrete goal of the meeting was to get the artists to sign up for individual interviews, where Tim and I would look at their portfolios and get to know them face to face. The only way for two people to interview two hundred people and ever get done is to set up an assembly line. So we asked every artist who wanted an interview to sign up for a fifteen-minute block of time one evening during the following two weeks. Nearly everyone at the meeting signed up, exceeding our most optimistic expectations (and when your most optimistic expectations are as optimistic as ours were, getting in the ballpark was an accomplishment). We were on our way.

Until the first evening of interviews. The first interview was scheduled for 5:00 the following Monday night. Nobody came. The second interview, scheduled for 5:15, was likewise one-sided. Nobody came at 5:30 or 5:45 either. Tim and I were in shock. We checked our schedules to see if we had somehow screwed up by scheduling the wrong night. Unfortunately, we hadn't.

At 6:16, just when we were about to go drink to excess, someone showed—the woman scheduled for 5:45. She was wearing a long, layered, wildly printed dress and, if I remember right, a turban. She introduced herself as Shambala, or some such nonsense name with affected astral overtones one runs into so often in Boulder. Very artsy, I thought optimistically— just what we need.

Then she showed us her portfolio. To this day I cannot believe her portfolio. The featured piece was a five-sided star, and a terrible one at that: slightly out of kilter, drawn with what looked to be a Bic pen, and xeroxed on a piece of cheap white paper. Tim and I looked at it for a long time, trying futilely to peel away any subtle layers of meaning. Finally we looked at each other, neither of us knowing quite what to say. All the while Shambala sat opposite, babbling on about the occult significance of the five-sided star, and how she always creates by candlelight, and just wait till we see what else she has for us.

What else she had for us turned out to be a series

of crude—I mean totally artless—scrawls. I remember something that looked like it might have been a flower; I think there was a drawing of—of all things—a bucket; and finally some pieces she called abstracts. ("I love to capture just what comes to mind," she said. "I hate to be a slave to reality.")

By this time Tim and I knew for certain that if old Shambala was anything, she was not a slave to reality.

The truly distressing aspect of this story is that the interviews didn't really get much better in the next two weeks. First of all, only about a third of the people who had committed to an interview even bothered to show up. And those who did show up were, for the most part, dismal disappointments. From our aspiring photographers we saw flat, muddy photograph after flat, muddy photograph of trees, dogs and friends making funny faces at the camera. From our aspiring illustrators we saw cartoon doodles, unfinished sketchbooks, and lots and lots of crude realism (the fledgling's favorite genre). But the worst group was, by far, the writers. Even people who know they can't do *anything* often don't know they can't write. In those two weeks I read enough banal headlines, sophomoric political manifestos, and bad stream-of-consciousness poetry to last me well into my next life.

To be fair, some of the people were good. They were there on time and had good stuff to show. And in truth we did come up with twenty or so whom we felt good enough about to include in the artists' cooperative... and, of them, about five who ultimately proved to be trustworthy members of the organization. But five, when we had planned for twenty-five, was not enough.

After three issues we folded the magazine.

You may think this was an extreme experience, and you're probably right. We were starting the kind of enterprise that attracts extreme people, in a town that attracts extreme people. Looking back, knowing what I know now, I see that it could not have worked out any other way.

But extreme or not, it taught me something that has since been borne out so many times I now consider it to be a watershed revelation. *Things that appear to be great—even flawless—in theory often don't work worth a damn.*

Owning My Own

So it was back to the drawing board...or in my case, the typewriter. I continued working part time at the publishing company and started thinking about what my next move would be. I didn't have to wait long. In the middle of one typical summer afternoon, as I was hard at work on a project, Peder (the owner of the company) came over and asked me to step into his office for a talk. For those of you who have never held a real job, here's a good rule: anytime your boss asks you into his office for "a talk," either something very good or something very bad is about to happen.

In this case, it was very good. Peder got right to the point: he asked me if I would like to have my own advertising agency, which he would finance as a silent partner, and I, as an active partner, would manage. His motivations were simple. "First, I like you and want to see you succeed," he said. "And second, I want you to make me a ton of money."

I was shocked, blown away, flattered...and somewhat unsettled. As I said earlier, I never had any dreams of owning my own business, at least not at that point of my life. On one hand, I thought the Grim Reaper had finally arrived to tie me down and make me commit to something. On the other hand, I knew it was an unbelievable opportunity. People with credentials, burning desire and starving families were selling their souls for venture capital. And here I was, having paid precious little dues, being approached by a guy who told me he believed in me and if I wanted my own business, he'd be glad to put up the money. It didn't make any sense.

But soon, as is the wont of unexpected opportunity, it felt karmic. Within a week I had accepted Peder's offer. And now, four years later, I can't imagine having it any other way.

Needless to say, I've learned a lot in the four years I've been in business. Much of it I will share with you in the following chapters. In the meantime you are going to get a much different account of the starting-out years from my co-author. Before Jimmy takes over, however, I would like to say one thing about him, because I think he's probably going to have trouble saying it about himself. Jimmy Calano is a phenom-enon, not only in terms of what he has accomplished for his age and the money he has earned, but in terms of the respect he has gained from the people he works with. His single most striking characteristic is his obsession with achievement. Most professionals have to struggle to keep a bottom-line orientation on the work they do, but with Jimmy it is second nature. When he doesn't know something he falls all over himself to learn it, enduring the most demoralizing, embarrassing mistakes until he has it mastered. And once he does have it mastered, he is relentless in putting it to productive use. His is a fascinating and most effective approach—one I've learned a lot from, and trust you will, too.

I'll let him tell the rest.

Jimmy

Nobody has ever made me do anything I didn't want to do—especially when I was a child.

First of all, I chose excellent parents who had both the means and inclination to give me everything a little boy could want. In return, I stayed out of trouble, and generally played the game by the rules. I was your typical pampered prince, the Silver Spoon Kid: well-behaved, but basically lazy.

In my first few years of school—that annoying intrusion on my TV-watching time—I took the approach that I would do only what was necessary to earn above-average grades. After all, I had to give my parents *something* to brag about. But I never worked hard. I was the one who did as little as possible and still made out okay.

There's no question that my childhood years were not too challenging...or productive, for that matter.

I have changed considerably. Looking back, I can identify several episodes which were central to my "transformation."

Super Joe

Back in 1969, when I was eleven years old, I remember turning on the TV one afternoon to find

Howard Cosell interviewing Joe Namath about the upcoming third Super Bowl. The game, between Namath's New York Jets and the opposing Baltimore Colts, was only three days away. It was considered to be *the* major event in professional sports that year.

I vividly remember the image: Joe Namath lounging by a pool, sporting those enormous dark sunglasses that were his trademark...flanked by two gorgeous blondes. When Cosell asked him the $64,000 "Who's gonna win?" question, Namath, with a coolness and cockiness I haven't seen since, replied, "We'll win, I guarantee you."

He was obviously the only one who thought so. In the conventional wisdom, the Jets didn't have a chance against the Colts. And the next day, sports writers jumped all over Namath for his brash comments. He had shot his mouth off and they went wild with the story. Most writers took the attitude of "Sure, Joe...sure you'll beat the Colts." And I remember feeling the same way.

Well, three days later in Super Bowl III, the New York Jets—led by Namath—did beat the Baltimore Colts...soundly. Sports fans were stunned. The media was blown away. And suddenly Joe Namath was a superstar. *Sports Illustrated* magazine re-nicknamed him from "Broadway Joe" to "Super Joe." In a January 20, 1969 cover story the magazine said, "It was called loudmouthing and bragging, but as it turned out, Super Joe told it the way it was. In a surprising display of passing accuracy and mental agility, he picked the Colt defense apart. He read the puzzling Colt defenses as easily as if they had been printed in comic books."

I was, as only an eleven-year-old can be, in awe.

Joe Namath was my childhood hero. Now I think I know why: he "told it like it was," without a flinch, hesitation or snag of self-doubt. And although winning an upset Super Bowl victory would have been more than enough to earn him a place in the record books, it is his style that has given him the "Babe Ruth" stature he now holds in professional football (and, for that matter, the celebrity status he holds generally).

Joe Namath was my first encounter with what I now call *kick-ass confidence,* a powerful concept Jeff and I will discuss a little later.

Going Private

Back to my schoolboy days. In seventh grade I transferred from a public elementary school, Sunset Ridge, to a conservative private school, Kingswood. I admit it, I was lured by the attraction of playing tackle football with pads and a *real* uniform—not the "superior" education, not the Ivy League environment, not the sprawling New England campus. With the change in schools I got considerably more than tackle football with pads and a real uniform. In public school I did next to nothing and got high grades. At Kingswood, however, I had to sweat just to pass. I went from being a "brain" to being a "dummy" overnight.

Eventually, though, I rose to meet the challenge. I found, to my surprise, that studying actually *can* improve one's grades. And I studied just enough to keep from flunking out. Besides, I was having too good a time playing tackle football with pads and a real uniform. After three years of living the life of an authentic "preppie," the principle lessons I had learned were arrogance, selfishness, and cockiness, par excellence. That's when I decided to switch back to a public high school. Remembering what a piece of cake my earlier public school experience had been, I was ready to be a "star."

Going Public

When I met with my public school guidance counselor, I insisted on taking the most demanding courses the school had to offer. I figured their toughest curriculum would offer me at least *some* challenge. Did it ever! My teachers were as good or better than *any* teacher I had had in private school. And most were more demanding. What I thought would be no challenge turned out to be no day at the beach. Once again, I had to work my tail off just to pass...and I was the kid with the exclusive prep school education!

I also had a big surprise on the playing field. After having gleaned two extra years of tackle football experience at a private school, I figured I'd show those public school boys a thing or two about the gridiron. That's not exactly what happened. Instead, I got my butt kicked—a lot—and learned for the first time what warming the bench was all about. After endless wind sprints, faithful suicide squad duty, and mending of pride, I earned a starting position by my senior year. I hung in there and eventually earned the respect of the other football players.

What was happening to me? Why was life suddenly so much work?

The "Do Something" Pep Talk
That Changed My Life

During the spring of my sophomore year (my first year back at public school) I tried out for the baseball team and got cut. Not too long after being officially "released," I decided to join the track team and try my luck in a "more individual" sport. (You couldn't get cut from the track team if you tried.)

The track coach, Mr. Baron, turned out to be my first mentor. You'd recognize him as the "Welcome Back Kotter" type in that he had excelled in athletics in high school, went off to college, and later returned to teach and coach at his old high school. He was a father figure to most of his students, and often coached us in life as well as athletics.

The most profound advice he ever imparted came during a team meeting before the biggest meet of the season. It went something like this: "So you guys all want to be Joe Hot Shot in school, right? You want to read your name in the newspaper? You want to hold court with the prettiest girls? You want everyone to be impressed? Do you really want these things?" (Hell, every guy in the room would have murdered his mother for them.) "Then it's simple. *Just do something.* That's all it takes."

His comments, of course, were in reference to the times, distances and heights we would strive for in the next day's meet. But beneath the surface I realized I'd been exposed to not just a pep talk, but a principle of life. Coach Baron's words made it crystal clear to me that winners are separated from losers simply by what they achieve. His philosophy made sense. And in the next three years it certainly held true: when

I scored well in a meet, all the glory and adulation flowed my way; when I did poorly, nothing happened and I remained unnoticed.

I've carried my coach's "do something" philosophy with me beyond high school athletic competition. In college, it was my inspiration to achieve high grades; in business, it's my central principle of success.

Academics Abound

As a high school junior, I developed, for the first time, serious scholastic discipline. Being in the top college-prep curriculum, I found myself in a scholastically competitive (I should say vicious) circle of peers. Until then I had been intensely competitive in other areas, like sports (tackle football with pads and a *real* uniform, remember?) but less so in school. Having "stepped down" from a private to a public school, there was no way I could allow myself to continue settling for passing grades while all my friends were getting *A*s. Plus, after suffering a humiliating sophomore year in athletics and academics, I felt the need to make a comeback.

So I met the competition head on and spent my final two years concentrating on reading, writing and 'rithmetic. It was tough. I had to bite the bullet, bear down, and make sacrifices I was unaccustomed to making. But when it was over I discovered that I could compete with the brightest of them—and hold my own. I realized I had what it took to meet the challenge.

During my three years in public high school, I went through a heavy transformation: from lethargic procrastination to hot intent. I was now a hard-

driving, conscientious student prepared to continue
my education at college. But I still had little concep-
tion of what the Real World was all about. Ready or
not, I was about to learn.

Off to College

Picture this. Midmorning in the late summer of
1975, having just returned from a three-week vacation in Paris, I was making a list of things to pack
for college. It was then that it hit me: "Life is good."
In one week, I would be heading off to Boulder,
Colorado to attend the University of Colorado. Rocky
Mountains. Sunny blue skies. Powder skiing.
Beautiful co-eds. Party campus... and total freedom
from family and responsibilities. I couldn't help thinking, "I've got it *made*."

So I was pretty smug when I left for college. Hey,
I'd learned how to be an achiever in high school; I had
the right stuff. And most of all, I had what I considered a major advantage over the majority of my
peers: I knew what I wanted to be when I grew up.

It was all planned. I would inherit my father's
retail furniture business after I graduated from college. Since childhood, this had been a "fact" of my life.
Not that I had resisted; actually, I *wanted* to take over
his company and be a second generation capitalist.
As early as I could remember I had hung around my
father's store preparing for my future stint as President of Calano Furniture, Incorporated. There was no
rebellion in me. My parents were living the American
Dream and you bet I wanted a piece of the action.

I can still remember driving halfway along the

2,000-mile trek from Hartford, Connecticut (my home town) to Boulder, somewhere on Route 80 on the highway plains of Iowa, happily recalling a conversation I had had a few months earlier with my father. I was sitting in his office after track practice late one afternoon when I gushed out the good news of my acceptance at CU. He, of course, was elated at having achieved another conspicuous success as a parent... and proceeded to give me a talk that I often repeated to myself. "Jimmy," he said, "when you get to college, have the time of your life. Make lots of friends, ski as often as you can, and make the most of your college years. Don't worry about grades, because people will only remember if you were a Phi Beta Kappa. Just get your degree. When you come back, the family business will be yours... *all* yours. You'll have a business waiting for you which will always provide you with The Good Life."

So there I was, driving off to college high on my "guaranteed future," anticipating four years of good times and not too much work (sort of the way Ronald Reagan must have felt when he left California for the White House). Yep, I was heading for a four-year Rocky Mountain high.

Easy Go

Would you believe *one* year? Within twelve months my father decided to close his twenty-three-year-old business. The economy had soured just as he was embarking on an expansion project and undertaking several new business ventures. Money tightened up, consumers stopped spending, and my father was caught leveraged beyond his equity position. In the end, he decided it would be best just to "close up" shop.*

When I returned home for summer vacation, the bad news was confirmed. I remember feeling like the son of a wealthy plantation owner returning home from the Civil War to find the plantation—and his future—in ruins. I was stunned. The life which had shaped my thinking was completely destroyed. Suddenly I had to confront—totally unprepared—the greatest fear of my life: having to prove to myself and the rest of society that I could cut it on my own. No hand-me-down business. No subsidies to help me get started. Nothing.

I was running scared.

A New Approach

I quickly changed course. Knowing there was no family business left to fall back on, I made two big decisions: to try to finish school in three years, and to not wait until I graduated before searching for my first job. Frankly, I figured the only way I now had a chance of succeeding in life was to get a jump on it.

I've since come to recognize this as a significant transition in my life: from being "reactive" to being "proactive." In the past, I had always just reacted to situations. Now I was taking initiative. Here's how I

---

*Within three years, though, my father rebuilt an entirely new and even more successful business. He learned well from his mistakes and maintained his optimism. A painful process for me to watch, it taught me the power of ambition and, yes, free enterprise. I know now I will never allow a setback to devastate me, because I know now it's really possible to make a comeback.

did it. I took advantage (in a positive sense) of a friend-ship I had cultivated with a certain professor. I idolized "the Doc"; he had a deliciously arrogant sense of humor, slick style, and tons of charisma. And I think he saw me as one of the business school's few bright and flashy (he liked flash) young hot shots. I became his teaching assistant. It was a great partnership: I kept the college administrators off his back for missing too many classes while he dashed around the country doing consulting work, and he let me play God in front of his freshman students.

When my family's business went under, I naturally went to talk to the Doc. If anyone could get me started, I figured he could, and I was certainly not too proud to ask.

It turns out that while I was confiding my fear and self-doubt to the Doc, another of his associates, Rick, was reveling in his first big-time success. A small-time consultant and entrepreneur, Rick had just achieved an outstanding success marketing national business seminars, and his company had gone from obscurity to national prominence in the field of continuing education. To initiate an expansion program, Rick needed to hire someone who could assist in coordi-nating the meeting planning logistics. While sharing the story of his new-found success, he had asked the Doc for the name of a conscientious student who might fit the bill. Guess who the Doc recommended? You got it. An interview date was set.

Count Your Successes

When the fog of failure is especially thick before your eyes, count your successes.
                                        —Sylvester Crane

By the time the interview rolled around I had counted my successes up, down and sideways. Ready with a verbal presentation to kill, I spent over two hours giving Rick testimony as to why no one on this earth was more suited for the job than I. I recited the minute details of every scholastic project I coordinated and every responsibility I held. I talked about anything that even remotely indicated I could excel in the position. I was obsessed with not blowing the opportunity. What I put on was a "dog and pony show" second to none.

At the conclusion of the interview, Rick offered me the job. What a relief! My actions that night—which I have yet to live down in some circles—give new meaning to the word *celebration*.

When my peers later attributed my instant success in the job market to "luck" or "being in the right place at the right time," I knew otherwise. I had created my own good fortune. By positioning myself as a loyal, dependable assistant with a well-known and admired professor/consultant, I had set myself up for success. At nineteen I had established a track record I was able to cash in on.

No Guts. No Glory.

The next two and a half years were my roughest yet. I was spread paper thin trying to maintain a respectable grade point average, work full time, remain active in a fraternity, finish college one year early, stay in touch with my family and friends, and feel good about it all at the same time. It wasn't easy.

Obviously, my college experience didn't turn out

to be what I had expected. But I have no regrets. I
could see when I took the job with Rick I was giving
up a lot—and if I couldn't see it, enough people certainly pointed it out to me. I saw that I was possibly
onto something big, and willingly made the decision
to get serious about my life a year or two early.

And it paid off. My new job was fabulous. I was
learning the process of producing business management seminars, dealing with high-powered people, and
traveling all over the country. Within two and a half
years, things were progressing nicely. The company
was going gang-busters, and I, now well established,
had a staff of four, an excellent salary, benefits,
bonuses, and lots of pride in my new career. I was routinely participating in decision-making activities and
even working independently with a few clients. At this
stage, no one had to tell me that my future—once
again—was exceptionally bright. I was a young turk
who had broken in on the ground floor of a company
that was mushrooming with success. Everything was
going just great.

And then I got fired.

The Ax

It was like getting kicked in the stomach. I was
shocked, furious, humiliated, and, ultimately,
devastated. Next to discovering that my family
business was out of business, getting canned was
about as bad as I've ever felt.

Maybe I should have seen it coming. But I didn't.
In my mind I had been the perfect employee: hardworking, dedicated, and effective. Rick, however, saw

it another way. From his perspective, I too often played the company's clients against the company, caused havoc with suppliers, took too many liberties, and was an inconsistent people manager. Also, I have a feeling I challenged Rick a few times too often on faults he didn't consider that important. In the last couple of years, as I've come to understand the ramifications of termination a little better (there's more on this subject later in the book), I've also come to appreciate Rick's point of view.

The final agreement he offered was as fair as any terminated employee could have expected. In fact, I have great respect for him, because he had the courage to do what he had to do—fire me—yet he did it with class. He told his clients, suppliers, and associates that I had "gone on to bigger and better things," and left the company on my own. That gesture enabled me to save face and move on without a stigma. (When you get fired, *everyone* wants to know why.)

Along with the graceful "resignation" I was allowed to fabricate, the financial package I received was equally generous: two months' severance pay and a huge bonus.

Easy Go...Again

Newly jobless, newly discouraged, and with a whole new nebulous future to worry about, I frantically grasped for what to do with the rest of my life. I narrowed my options to one: I wanted to continue working, in some capacity, with the clients I had dealt with at my previous job. These clients included lawyers, doctors, authors and top management executives who, because I was trained, dependable and understood their accounts backward and forward, all had left the door open for a future working relationship. In the past, several had even given me an outright invitation to come "on board" if I ever left my old company. I must say I just about lurched at each offer. (I was so scared I even enrolled in MBA classes!)

But deep down I knew I didn't want to work exclusively for any of these clients. And after some soul-searching, I realized I no longer wanted to work for *anyone*. Just me. Sure, it was a high-risk option, but I figured I was young enough to fall flat on my face and still have my whole life in front of me.

So I went to my ex-boss and proposed that as part of my severance package, he break off a small portion of one account (his largest) to help me get started in my own business. I wisely chose an area of the account that required endless legwork, complex details, constant traveling, and tedious follow-up. As expected, he was only too happy to divest that part of the account and let me deal with the client directly. Again, a matter of perspective: to him it was a service that required too much time and returned too little profit; to me it was the foundation of my first company.

So with my tidy deal in hand, I set up shop in my second bedroom and declared myself in business. After deliberating about thirty seconds, I decided to name the business Calano & Company. I had only one partial client, but with my severance money I had enough dough to keep me going until I got rolling. And that didn't take long.

A week later I contacted a previous client I had done independent consulting for. I suggested he retain me on a regular basis to produce his seminar. He accepted my proposal, and I now had client number two.

About two months later, a long-standing client of my old company was resigned by my ex-boss. They in turn decided to handle their own account and asked if I'd be interested in helping them on a free-lance arrangement. Why, of course...Client number three.

Good things were starting to happen. But I didn't spring into the "major leagues" until six months later. That happened when my old company unexpectedly broke ties with the client I had a part of, and I ended up with the entire account. At first I thought it was a gift from paradise. Later, a "lucky break." But now I realize I got the account because I earned it. Having worked closely with the client while at my old company, I came to understand the account in great depth. And without realizing it, I had established a track record in their eyes. Furthermore, after getting fired I had continued to perform a number of extra services for them, even though I wasn't being paid. I never pitched the account, or tried to steal it from my old company, but certain critical tasks weren't getting done properly, and I had always been there to fill the gaps. What started as only a partial account was now a major account that gave me the financial resources and stability to expand my company.

Thinking Big...Finally

So, my life and career were really opening up. Within nine months of getting fired I had established myself in a small but flourishing business, just as I had wanted. I remember thinking at the time, "This is too good to be true, it can't get any better." But it did.

At my old company, one of the responsibilities I most enjoyed was ordering mailing lists. (These are the lists of names and addresses of people to whom we mail our brochures promoting the seminars.) I did this through a sister company, and, after nearly three years of purchasing lists, I had developed a specialty skill essential to the marketing of the seminars. With my new company, however, I had no occasion to use it. That changed when one of my clients offered to give me his mailing list business if I would agree to set up a mailing list brokerage firm. Would I! I instantly reasoned that this was a wonderful opportunity to offer a new service to my clients, continue doing what I had enjoyed in my last job, and increase my profits in the process. Plus, it would make a perfect ancillary business to my seminar production company. My client's offer was a golden opportunity which I wasted no time in seizing.*

Even though the list business is characterized as tedious and detail-oriented, the trade-off is that it's also highly profitable, provided you have a steady clientele that purchases a large volume of lists. That was what I was after. It wasn't long before my newly formed company, Execulists, began handling, one by one, the mailing list purchases for Calano & Company's seminar clients. It was the perfect blend of

---

*I always thought I deserved to be in the *Guinness Book of World Records* for the rapidity with which I set up my second corporation, Execulists, Inc. I had a telephone number, logo designed, stationery printed, and corporation papers processed all in about two weeks. Now that's turnaround!

services. Each business was 100% independent, yet complemented the activities of the other, ultimately serving my clients more thoroughly.

The combined profits of my two companies were enough to afford me the financing and confidence to expand my operations. Eight months after my second business was rolling along, I opened an office suite in one of Boulder's newest business complexes, added two staff members, and took on three new clients. At twenty-three, I had founded and built two companies which generated over $500,000 in combined revenues in their first full year of operation. Beginner's luck, I guess.

Meeting Jeff

The first brutal realization I had to deal with during this tender phase of my career was that I could not be as good as I wanted to be at everything I wanted to be good at. I had envisioned myself as a seminar producer, media specialist, marketing consultant, advertising copywriter, meeting planner and entrepreneur. But, alas, it was time to learn there wasn't time to do them all, and I wasn't as good at some things as I thought I was. When I had finally begun to accept this reality (it was hard), I met Jeff. Before I tell about that, however, let me back up a moment.

My first certified flop in business was a pilot seminar on a sizzling hot topic, stress management, which I produced from scratch for a client. I wrote the copy, designed the mailing piece, selected the mailing lists, handled the production, chose the test cities, coordinated the meeting logistics, and oversaw every last detail of the entire project. Although my client and friends were impressed with my efforts, and assured me the pilot would be a smashing success, it wasn't. It bombed. That was when I realized I needed outside expertise.

So, with the help of my ever-creative and dependable free-lance graphic designer, Bob Byrd, I recruited an unknown (to me) copywriter by the name of Jeff Salzman to rewrite the copy in my client's failed brochure. Admitting I wasn't a "good enough" copywriter was awful at first, but once I saw what a truly professional writer could deliver, I was angry at myself for not having sought outside help in the first place. The work Jeff did on my client's brochure was brilliant. He turned a big loser into a big winner, and saved me a client. (Thanks, Jeff.)

After that success, Jeff and I continued to work closely on many projects, leading up to this book. But you've heard the expression "nothing lasts forever" and *our* honeymoon came to a sudden halt when the seminar/training industry to which we provided our services began to go sour.

During the 1981–1982 recession, money was tight and most companies were forced (from stockholder pressure) to reduce their training budgets. When training budgets dried up, people stopped going to seminars and our clients stopped sponsoring them. For Jeff and me, this meant no more meeting planning, no more copywriting, and no more list ordering. As our clients began withdrawing from the marketplace, Jeff's and my services were no longer in such hot demand.

To make matters worse, I got fired by one of the

few remaining clients we shared. When that happened, I did something irrational and desperate: I decided to form my own training company. (You'll find that business success is often the result of an eleventh-hour, last ditch maneuver.) Heck, going on my own worked the last time I got fired, why not now? At first Jeff thought I was nuts, but when I offered him a fifty-fifty partnership, he suddenly thought my idea made a lot more sense.

My rationale was this: we had made several of our clients wealthy in the course of our relatively short careers, so why couldn't we do the same for ourselves? All we had to do was risk losing a lot of money we didn't have, convince several suppliers to give us credit we didn't deserve, and maybe invest some time with no pay-off. Given the potential returns (and the fact that our clients were dropping like flies), we decided we didn't really have a choice. Jeff came up with the company name, CareerTrack, and we were in business.

The first seminar we produced with our company was directed to the professional woman's market, a market we had sold to successfully with our past clients. We titled the seminar "Image and Self-Projection."

Jeff wrote the copy, I ordered the mailing lists, Jeff's art director, a man named T, designed the brochure, and my assistant, Annie, handled all the paperwork. We were all wildly optimistic about the potential returns (and, of course, about having a second chance during bad times), but we were also terrified of a bomb. With hopes high, our bank account long past drained and our nerves frazzled, we mailed our first brochures and prayed.

The returns were staggering. Our first time at bat we hit a grand slam home run. When all the responses were tallied, we had tripled the industry standard for response and earned a huge profit. More importantly, we had laid the groundwork for what is now the fastest growing company in the training industry. In the fifteen short months following our pilot program, "Image and Self-Projection," God love it, has become the single most popular professional woman's workshop in the country. We've grown to over thirty-five employees, sixteen trainers, five additional seminars and over five million dollars in sales. It's incredible; so incredible sometimes, frankly, Jeff and I look at each other and say "is this really happening to us?"

And Now...

Looking back, I see the transformations I've undergone as a series of "rising to meet the challenge" episodes: from "easy" public school to demanding private school; from private school back to public school; from the freedom of college to the reality of the Real World; and, from working for someone else to working for myself, I gained the confidence to set my goals higher and go after them with more vigor each time around.

And right now I'm sitting here at my desk reflecting on how it feels to be where I am. I've got the money, the dream home, the cars, the clothes and the "executive toys," and when I think about it, I realize that I'm well on my way to what has been hyped as the Great American Dream. But I also realize that these things do not constitute my success, they only represent it.

I've often noticed how people who don't have all the amenities that a successful career affords tend to trivialize them. I'm sure you've heard (and maybe even made) comments like, "I don't need those things to be happy." Well I don't need them to be happy, either. But I've got them, and as Dudley Moore, in the movie *Arthur,* said to the shopkeeper who asked him how it felt to have 750 million dollars, *"It feels great."*

Aside from the ego gratification that comes from the money and the lifestyle, I'm most proud of the success itself. All the other stuff is terrific, and I enjoy it, but the one thing that keeps me energized is the sense of accomplishment I feel. Admittedly, I'm probably no happier now than when I was a child, but the self-respect I've earned through my career has enhanced my satisfaction with life.

If I Could Do It, You Can Do It

And lastly, for the record I want you, the aspiring professional, to know that I attribute my success to no "wealth formula," no lucky break (breakthroughs, yes, but breaks, no), no rich uncle, no family business, no answered prayers, no accident. Just the all-American virtues of goal-setting, ambition, conscientious effort, hard work and persistence. It's in vogue these days to say, "There's no easy way to make it," and I'm going to say it: There's no easy way to make it. So dig in your heels, because it's your turn at bat. Hit a home run.

If I could do it, you can do it.

3: College Daze: The Young Professionals Look Back

Ask people who have been in the workaday world for a few years what they remember about college, and invariably they'll start talking about the wild times, the fun, the pranks, the liberation. The quickest way to shut them up is to ask them what they learned in the classroom.

That's because they didn't learn very much. And you probably didn't either. It's not that college is a waste of time. All the fun and freedom serves an important purpose. College is society's great halfway house, a safe, semistructured place to pass those dangerous post-high-school years when we all have so much growing up to do. However, this is generally viewed as incidental to the larger purpose of college, which is to make us smarter. At that, unfortunately, college is a dismal failure. Although most people leave college wiser, almost nobody leaves college smarter.

That's why you should realize right now that as a fresh college graduate you are not nearly as prepared for a job in the professional world as you may think. The people who will be hiring you know it, the people you will be working with know it, and you might as well know it, too. The American institution of higher education is in bad shape, and one of the most important things you must do to prepare yourself for a professional career is understand the three major ways college has failed you.

1. The professors are generally lousy. Before we indiscriminately indict an entire profession, let us say that many college professors are talented, committed and competent professionals. What is more important, however, is that many of them are terrible. In fact, so many of them are so terrible that the overall quality of instruction at the college level is appallingly bad.

In a way it's no wonder. Professors today make, on the average, $23,650 a year.* Comparably trained professionals in the nonacademic professions can make thousands of dollars—often tens of thousands— more. That's why universities seldom attract high-level talent away from the Real World. As a result, the only reasons anyone sticks with academia are 1) the opportunity to teach, and possibly inspire, counts for more than money, or 2) he or she couldn't cut it outside the ivory tower. The second is far more often the case.

Another reason the quality of instruction is so low in college is that there is little incentive for professors to excel. They are rarely checked or critiqued—and in the case of tenured professors it wouldn't matter if they were. (Down with tenure! Who else in society

---

*According to the *Wall Street Journal*, September 1981.

has it?) It is just too easy to slough off when there is no pressure or external expectation to do anything else. Sure, professors can get recognition by publishing papers and doing research, but as you've probably realized by now, good researchers are not necessarily good teachers. In fact, in our experience, the two skills are *inversely* proportional.

The University of Colorado (Jimmy's alma mater) instituted a professorial grading system several years ago that has helped increase professional account-ability. It's a relatively simple system that could be implemented at virtually any college (and probably has been at many). The system works like this: at the end of each semester students fill out forms rating various aspects of each course and professor they had; the results are printed and distributed just prior to the next enrollment period. At the moment, that's the extent of it. It's simply a public opinion tool, a way of exposing the best and the worst for all to see. It would be interesting to see what would happen if the ratings were taken a step further, and made an ele-ment of a system determining a professor's salary and promotions. You can bet there would be an instant increase in the quality of education. Some people argue that this would turn teaching into a popular-ity contest. But they underestimate the fairness of students, and ignore the fact that college is a business, and students, as consumers, have certain rights.

At Brown University's 1981 commencement, Pro-fessor Jacob Neusner gave another view of professorial popularity:

> We the faculty take no pride in our educational
> achievements with you...With us you could argue

about why your errors were not errors, why mediocre work really was excellent, why you could take pride in routine and slipshod presentation. For four years we created an altogether forgiving world, in which whatever slight effort you gave was all that was demanded. When you did not keep appointments, we made new ones. When your work came in beyond deadline, we pretended not to care.

Why? Despite your fantasies, it was not even that we wanted to be liked by you. It was that we did not want to be bothered, and the easy way out was pretense: smiles and easy *B*s.

Few professors actually care whether or not they are liked by peer-paralyzed adolescents, fools so shallow as to imagine professors care not about education but about popularity. It was, again, to be rid of you. So go, unlearn the lies we taught you.*

Interesting.

2. Standards are sinking. Anyone who thinks college isn't a business should ask himself or herself why grades are so high and standards are so low. It isn't because of "educational democratization" or "creative curricula" or anything quite so high-minded. It's because colleges, like the Greyhound Bus Company, are in the business of filling seats. And the only way they can fight the forces of a declining market is to make the ride more comfortable.

Anyone who has ever gone to college secretly suspects that he or she could have done a notch above nothing and still gotten by. We've all had "fresh air" (a.k.a. "breeze") courses that we crammed into two

*Taken from *Forbes Magazine*, October 26, 1981.

nights: the night before the midterm and the night before the final. It's the Big Inside Joke: the only people who still have a high regard for college are the ones who didn't get to go.

In fact, in some undergraduate schools today a student can maintain full academic standing with a *D* average. For students, as for professors, it's hard to do much when so little is expected. The situation is essentially the inverse of the old maxim: "When the tide goes up, all boats rise." In this case the tide goes down and all boats fall—although, uncannily, none of them ever seems to sink.

The big push for group work is another factor in the decline of higher education. The ambitious, bright students too often do their own work and more, while the lazy, less competent ones do little and look great. The purpose of group work is admirable—certainly we all need to learn to work together—but in practical terms the purpose is seldom achieved. Instead, the hard workers work harder and the lazies get away with it.

Pass/fail is another waste. Has anyone ever given 100% in a pass/fail course? Why bother? It's like competing in the 100-yard dash and opting to walk: the objective becomes to just cross the finish line. The pass/fail option is a university's way of telling students it's okay to slide by.

And then there's the problem that dares not speak its name: cheating. We once saw a statistic showing that over 90% of all college students have cheated. If you were one of them—and be honest with yourself—just be aware that to whatever degree you cheated you have undermined your professional capabilities.

3. The emphasis is on facts, not skills. College courses tend to concentrate on providing students with hard information, as if the knowledge that is important in a particular field never changes. Jimmy recalls a chemistry professor who required his students to memorize the periodic table of elements...which is printed in any encyclopedia, many dictionaries, and the endsheets of almost any chemistry book you can find. Why would anyone ever need to memorize it? Similarly, Jeff graduated with a degree in journalism without ever having learned to type—although he learned quite well the principles of hot-lead typesetting, a technique that was completely superseded by a computer-based process in the early 1970s.

This facts-based approach to education is more than wasteful, it is downright destructive. It leads students to think that upon graduating from college they have been "educated," that they have learned virtually all they will ever need to know to succeed in their profession. It closes, rather than opens, the mind.

A better approach, more suited to our world of mushrooming information, would be to teach students the *skills* necessary to cope with the evolving professional environment. This skills-oriented approach would teach processes rather than events. A skills-oriented business curriculum, for instance, might include subjects such as negotiation, self-presentation, leadership, listening, time management, coping with change, stress management, creative thinking, and computer consciousness. An understanding of these areas would prepare students for any non-technical contingency they're apt to face.

How to Make the Most of the College You Have Left

All is not lost...yet. If you have some time to kill before graduating, you have a chance to provide yourself with some of the education college has not been able to give you. Here are three relatively simple ways to go about it:

1. Get an internship. Or better yet, get a job (they pay better). Most professionals will tell you they learned more about their profession during their first year on the job than in all their years of college. Why not get some of that Real World learning under your belt right now? The options are limitless.

Suppose you're in marketing. You could learn a lot by conducting, or assisting with, a market research project for a new business in your town. Most new businesses would be happy to have help in this complex area, even if it's just for a "second opinion." Sure, you've probably solved marketing case problems in your textbooks, but authentic problems will teach you skills your textbooks couldn't even approach, such as: how to use nonuniversity information resources, how to deal with managers who have no clear idea what their marketing problems are, how to make a decision on the basis of insufficient data (a common and critical Real World problem that college rarely addresses), and how to handle the spate of unexpected problems that pop up on any nonacademic project.

This learn-by-doing approach is valuable in virtually any field. If you're in medicine, you could offer your services to a local hospital. If you want to be a teacher, look into day-care work. If you're in political science, try working on the election campaign of a local official.

Even if you work for no pay, it is still preferable to what you've been doing: paying your professors for the opportunity to do work that is far less valuable. Also—and we can't emphasize it enough—this kind of initiative looks *fabulous* on your resume. It sets you apart from the vast majority of students who get out of college without having ever set foot in the environment of which they expect to be a part.

2. Interview. Take advantage of the droves of interviewers that pass through your campus every semester. You don't have to be particularly interested in working for their companies, but the interviews themselves will give you the practice and feedback you need to make the interviews you eventually *are* interested in count. By the way, don't wait until your last semester to begin this process. The first semester of your junior year is not too soon to start. We will discuss the *process* of interviewing in detail in the next chapter.

3. Counsel with professionals. People who have been successful in a profession you're interested in can give you insights you would never get in a classroom...and most of them would be flattered to have the opportunity. Think of them as walking resources.

If you're interested in investigating the architecture profession, for instance, find an architect who is doing the kind of work that appeals to you (check with the chamber of commerce, a local association of architects, or the American Institute of Architects), and ask him or her to meet with you. The best approach is to send a letter first and follow-up with a phone call. The initial letter is important; it should read something like this:

Ms. Juliet Phillips, President
Phillips & Arnold, Inc.
123 Smith Boulevard
Clarion, CA 93097

Dear Ms. Phillips,

    My name is Ann Morgan. I am a student
at Clarion University considering a career in
architecture. I know that you are quite successful in the profession (I am a fan of your First
National renovation), and would like to have
the opportunity to get an "insider's" point of
view from you.

    Would you agree to a brief meeting with
me? Perhaps I could take you to lunch one day
the week of May 19th. I know you are very
busy, and I would appreciate any time you
could give me. I'll call you in a few days to see
if this is possible.

    Thanks for your consideration.

        Sincerely,

        Ann Morgan

    Notice that this letter contains three important
elements: 1) Ann let Ms. Phillips know that she was
familiar with and appreciated her work, 2) Ann did
not just assume that Ms. Phillips would agree to the
request, and 3) Ann invited Ms. Phillips to lunch—a
token "exchange" for the value that Ann places on
the meeting. Lunch is a good idea because the professional is far more likely to relax and give you the
attention you want if you meet outside his or her

office. Also lunch represents a finite amount of time, so no one feels "trapped."

At the meeting ask your subject good, open-ended questions: *What do you like best about your profession? What do you like least? How do you get work and how does it flow through your organization? What are the typical problems you face day to day? What advice can you give me?* Chances are he or she will get as much of a new perspective as you will. Perhaps you could even ask to visit his or her office for a day, doing an odd job or just observing what goes on. This kind of hands-on investigation is invaluable, particularly if you are not sure of the profession you want to enter.

One of the most important benefits you could get from this interview is that your "professional counselor" might become your mentor, or even your future employer. If you approach him or her properly, you will make a strong and lasting impression.

4: Knowing Where You're Going

You are about to enter the most exciting phase of your life so far. All your years of preparation are over. You have been fully bred, weaned and schooled, and now you are ready, presumably, to put it all to the test. Ready or not, it's time to go.

You are about to embark on what Daniel Levinson* calls the "Entering the Adult World" phase of life. This is a distinct and predictable period of adult life that generally lasts until our early thirties, at which time we either tear it down or shore it up for the next phase. This young adult life-phase is characterized by two conflicting forces: one is the desire to build solid foundations; the other is the desire to keep things flexible. In other words, we want to "go for it" and at the same time "hang loose."

---

*Daniel Levinson's landmark, ten-year study *Seasons of a Man's Life* has done for the understanding of the stages of adulthood what Jean Piaget did for the understanding of the stages of childhood.

It's a fierce conflict and it manifests itself in every facet of our lives. On one hand we want to make solid career progress, and on the other hand we want to avoid limiting ourselves or "selling out" to a particular company or profession. We want the security of our families and we want independence. We want to be liked and we want to make a stand. We want the fulfillment of an exclusive love relationship and we want to hop into bed with everything we see.

Obviously we can't have it both ways, right? Well no, in some ways we absolutely *can* have it both ways. And in fact we owe it to ourselves to *try* to have it both ways. Perhaps the biggest misconception fresh graduates have is that the choices they make are irrevocable, that every decision is a lifetime commitment. We've been trained to think that way. All our lives we've been "building for the future," and as a result we tend to see each move we make as one more step firmly in the direction of The Goal. Unfortunately, most of us don't have any idea what The Goal is; therefore, the idea of making irrevocable steps in *any* direction is terrifying. For some people it is immobilizing; paralyzed by their inability to make the "right" decisions, they end up making no decisions at all. For others it is demoralizing, and they shuffle quietly into the lifecourse of least resistance, resigned for the rest of their lives to making the most of it.

Certainly some of the decisions we make now may limit our options for the rest of our lives (and all of them will in varying degrees *color* the rest of our lives). But for the most part, it is not only unnecessary but unreasonable to expect that upon graduating from college we know enough about ourselves and the world to map out an immutable, long-term course. This is particularly true for our generation. We are faced today with an array of options unimaginable in our parents' generation. The young adult lifephase is our time to explore these options and to let our explorations change us. It is the "fitting room" of life, our chance to try on different careers, partners, values, lifestyles and personas to see how they feel and look before we lay our money down.

This doesn't mean we should steer clear of commitment. On the contrary, making strong commitments is necessary to fulfill the "option-testing" purpose of this lifephase. Testing an option is like testing a light bulb: unless you give it all the energy it requires, you'll never know whether it would have worked or not. The point is not to make weak commitments, but to put commitment in a more mature perspective—by developing the confidence and courage to adjust or abandon a commitment that you decide is unsound, and by understanding that change is inevitable and failure can be constructive.

When Jeff asked his former boss Wilson, on Wilson's fortieth birthday, how it felt to turn forty, he answered, "Getting older is the process of limiting your options, and it feels good." We suspect it does. In the meantime, however, the road between flexibility and commitment is full of bumps—and even a few land mines. But like it or not, it's the only road that goes anywhere. In the following pages we will share some insights and techniques that will make the going a little easier.

Setting Goals

*It's too hard, and life is too short, to spend your
time doing something because someone else has said
it's important. You must feel the thing yourself.*
                                        —Isidor I. Rabi

We all have to have goals in order to do anything.
It's obvious: if we don't know where we want to go, how
will we know in which direction to move? How will we
know how close we are, or even when we've arrived?

Goals enable us to manage, whether we are managing a business, a Little League team or ourselves. They
set the direction and measure the movement of our
lives. The big misconception about goals is that once
they are set they must be achieved. But falling short of
a goal does not necessarily constitute failure, at least
not total failure. With goals, the process can be as valuable as the result...and of course, in those cases where
the result is never achieved, much more valuable.

The most important purpose of setting goals is not
achievement, but self-knowledge. By finding out what
we want we also find out who we are. Finding out what
you want may at first sound like a pretty easy exercise:
you want a new car, you want to go to sleep, you want
a candy bar, you want to go out for a drink. If anything,
you may think you'd be better off if you thought a little
less about what you want. But knowing what you want
on a short-term, day-to-day basis is a lot different from
knowing what you want out of life.

The latter is a whole other exercise. It's scary. In
fact, it's so scary that many people purposely keep
themselves busy with the *wants* of life as a means of
distracting themselves from having to face the *goals*
of life. They build careers, raise families, and go merrily

through the motions without ever questioning whether what they are getting is what will really fulfill them. Maybe they fear self-knowledge will lead them to the conclusion that fulfillment requires dismantling their present life, and constructing a new one. What they don't know is that people who have done that success-fully are among the happiest people on earth.

So while setting goals may be scary, it is necessary. Because if you don't have the courage to pursue your own goals, you will leave yourself open to the multitude of people who will be only too happy to recruit you to pursue theirs.

The Twenty-Year Fantasy Session

An effective way to define your long-term goals is to go on what we call a *Twenty-Year Fantasy Session*. The purpose of this exercise is not to lock yourself into an airtight lifeplan. Rather, it is meant to enable you to get yourself moving in a certain direction, and give you a means to measure your progress.

The Twenty-Year Fantasy Session requires some preparation. You must set aside a good block of time, at least an entire morning, afternoon or evening, preferably in a neutral, undistracting environment (it's great for vacations or a free day). Other than that all you will need is a pen and paper.

Phase One of the Twenty-Year Fantasy Session involves simply creating mental images of your future. The only rules are that you 1) create these images around discrete periods of your life: one year from now, two years, five years, ten years, fifteen years, and twenty years; 2) take a Gestalt approach and include in your image every aspect of your life: career, personal, lifestyle, spiritual and family; and 3) write down your images on paper.

Think of the Twenty-Year Fantasy Session as an exercise not in *developing* your goals, but in *uncovering* and *identifying* the goals that are already there— as a simple result of your being the person you are. It's as if you were trying to slip unnoticed into your own soul. This is not any easy thing to do; like most people you have probably gone to great lengths to keep some of your desires safely hidden. And though some of them may well deserve to stay hidden, the point of this exercise is to bring up for discussion as much as possible.

Keep in mind that the Twenty-Year Fantasy Session is just an exercise; it does not mean anything you don't want it to mean. The key is to adopt an open-to-anything mind-set. Let your images flow freely, without criticism and evaluation. Write down everything that pops into your mind. You'll have plenty of time to interpret and edit later on.

Start by recording all your latest daydreams, the ones you've been entertaining during classes, and confiding to your closest friends. When those are exhausted, change perspective, and instead of looking into the future try looking into the past. Imagine yourself on your deathbed. *What would you have wanted to accomplish to make your life worthwhile?* Or think back to when you were a kid. *What did you want to be when you grew up? What was the happiest you've ever been? What is the most fun you've ever had?* You will be amazed at how fast your thinking crystallizes.

Don't fantasize just about what you want to do and have, but also about who you want to *be.* Imagine that you are about to have dinner with the person you will be in twenty years. *What do you expect this person to be like? What will you talk about? Do you like him or her? Does he or she seem happy? What advice will he or she want to give you?* These are all excellent mechanisms for getting the fantasies flowing.

Now for the hard part. After you have some good images on paper, put them aside and start over. Lead yourself on a completely new line of thinking. This step is important because it gives you a chance to step back from your established expectations and look around at all your other options. You may not otherwise allow yourself to do this. Like most people, you are probably afraid of the thought of violating the lifescript in which you have already invested so much in terms of time, momentum and lost opportunities. In fact, you may think your options are pretty limited. But let's take George Bernard Shaw's word for it: youth is wasted on the young. In our twenties we have options like we will never have again. Use the Twenty-Year Fantasy Session as a safe, noncommital opportunity to look at them.

After you have fantasized all your options from all the different perspectives, and written it all down, the next step is to make sense of it. You are ready to move into Phase Two of the Twenty-Year Fantasy Session: evaluation. The purpose of this phase is to translate your stream-of-consciousness imagery into discrete, mentally manageable goals. The best approach is to look at your fantasies critically from the following three perspectives.

1. Are they realistic? This is a tough question. Is it unrealistic to set the goal of becoming President of the United States? Making a million dollars by age thirty? Living in Tahiti? Achieving oneness with the universe? Only you can decide what is realistic for you. But at this point in your life it is better to set your goals unrealistically high than to sell yourself out by setting them too low.

2. Are they compatible? It is probably a mistake to set your sights on achieving a Ph.D. and financial independence *both* by age thirty. However, it's entirely possible that you could have both by age forty. Many goals that seem mutually exclusive at first glance may not be. Remember, multiple careers will be the norm for our generation. It may be perfectly reasonable to expect that you could, at various points in your life, be a successful corporate lawyer, do volunteer work in the Third World, and live a quiet, artist's life in the country.

3. Are they measurable? State your goals in objective, measurable terms. For instance, don't settle for the goal of being "well-read." Define what well-read means. If you decide it means you should read fifty books a year, then you know you must read an average of one a week. At that point you know whether the goal is attainable, whether its achievement requires a speed reading course (which then becomes another goal), whether it should take priority over other goals, or whether it ought to be adjusted. And equally important, every week you will be able to measure your progress.

Putting It in Order

The final phase of the Twenty-Year Fantasy Session consists of placing your *realistic, compatible* and *measurable* goals into chronological order over the next twenty years of your life. Those goals which seem most attainable should be slotted for achievement within the next few years; the intermediary ones should be placed in the mid-phase; and those which require experience and heavy credentials should be positioned toward the latter part of the twenty-year span (you can always move them up).

Devise a master plan in one-year, two-year, five-year, ten-year, and twenty-year increments. After twenty years, things start getting pretty foggy, so don't worry about projecting any further. Besides, what you do in the next twenty years will determine to what degree you reach any of your goals, because that is when your patterns and approaches to goal achievement will be formed. If you develop an effective approach, you might achieve most of your lifetime goals within the next twenty years, thereby opening up a whole new future. On the other hand, if you develop ineffective ones you may never achieve much of anything within the next *fifty* years.

Be sure you use your masterplan. Bring it out every few months for an evaluation and update. Do you still want to achieve all those goals? How much progress have you made? What have been your major barriers and hang-ups? What deletions, additions, or adjustments do you want to make?

Every time you look at your master plan you will want to make adjustments. This is a natural result of maturing and focusing on what is important. Make changes freely. Remember, setting goals is just as important as achieving them. It would be uncanny if your goals remained constant throughout your life. By the way, it's a nice idea to keep your old master plans. They make a good record of your feelings and ambitions at various points in your life.

Now, close this book and go on your own Twenty-Year Fantasy Session.

Knowledge is Transferable

It's likely that even after having successfully set goals, you are not going to have a clear idea of what your first step should be toward reaching them.

Therefore you may be tempted, like so many college graduates, to take a dead-end, makeshift job at $12,000 a year until the "dream job" comes along. But that can be a real trap. Too often years go by in your makeshift job and nothing happens. Sooner or later your luck runs out as you begin to lose your image of being a fresh graduate/aspiring professional and still have no experience in your field. Some people hang on to the dead-end job because it's easy not to work hard—after all, it's not a "real" job—or simply because they are reluctant to stop being a teenager. But all a future employer will care about is that you didn't make your career happen then, and you probably won't now.

Don't fall into the waiting-for-the-ultimate-job trap. The ultimate job will never find you; you must find it. If you are unable to decide on a career direction you should narrow your choices to career paths that look most attractive, and get a job—any job—at the earliest possible point. In other words, *do the first thing that sounds remotely interesting.*

For example, say you know you want to go into business, but aren't sure in what capacity. In that case you could take a job as an insurance salesperson. (By the way, this is a great field in which to get a high-potential first job.) One of five things will happen:

1. At the very worst you will find out, unequivocally, that selling insurance is not for you. If so, you've made good progress: you will never have to consider this career as an option again.

2. You may not like selling insurance policies, but may find that you are drawn to a totally different area of the insurance business, such as management, administration or claims resolution. Your experience in sales will have helped you understand, firsthand, an important area of the business. This will make you a more viable management candidate. You may even transfer within your company and utilize the knowledge gleaned from your sales experience to step ahead of other management trainees.

3. You think being an insurance salesperson is not so great, but being in sales is. If so, find a product or service you could get excited about representing. "Spinning off" like this will enable you to transfer all the sales skills you developed while pushing policies.

4. You may *love* selling insurance. The role fits you and gives you the rewards you were looking for. Terrific! You have made a quantum leap in building a career foundation. In the insurance business, the sooner you get started the sooner you build up a portfolio of policies, and the sooner you start making lots of money.

5. You're only moderately satisfied with selling insurance. It's a good, comfortable living, but not what you were ultimately looking for. Here is where the unexpected may occur (sometimes with your help). You get a break. This happened to Nick, a friend of Jimmy's. Nick represented Metropolitan Life for many years. During this period he developed a good sales style and earned a reputation for being a dependable, honest, personable businessman. But despite having achieved conspicuous success as an insurance agent, he was not entirely satisfied with his career. That's why he was able to walk away from it when one of his clients, who was impressed with Nick's abilities as an insurance agent, offered him a public relations position with a highly respected plastics company. Being the "front man" for his new company was the perfect opportunity for Nick to transfer the "people skills" he developed so well as an insurance sales-person to a new field he liked a lot better. (After all, as an insurance salesman, he had been dealing with people on a delicate—level convincing them that they will die someday.)

In his new job Nick works five days a week traveling and entertaining clients, and he loves it. The clincher is that he is still being paid commissions on every active policy he wrote during the years he sold insurance. He not only enjoys a substantial salary, expense account and benefits from his new company, but also a steady income from his previous career.

The point is, don't let not finding the "dream job" right off the bat keep you from getting started. As Jimmy's high school track coach said, "Just do something." Even if it's wrong, you're bound to learn from it, and that knowledge will be transferable to later tasks. When you're unsure, diving right in is usually your best move. It will open up a whole new world of options.

5: Scoring The Ultimate Job

You know the whole sad story. Uncle Sam does not want you. The American economy is hurting. Millions of people—experienced and dependable people—still wait to be called back to work, yesterday's boom companies have implemented hiring freezes, there's a two-hour line at the unemployment office, teachers are waiting tables, biologists are driving cabs. For the first time ever in America it seems that a college education does not guarantee the Good Life. And you, poor recent graduate, are worse off than most. Since you were born at the wrong end of the baby boom, your older brothers and sisters have already divvied up the entry-level jobs. You're last in line at the famine.

That's the bad news. The good news is that as bad as the bad news is, it doesn't have to matter. There are plenty of good jobs out there. In fact, employers (like us, for instance) are moaning because there aren't enough "good people" to fill the good jobs that *are* available.

So if there are people without jobs, and jobs without people, what's wrong?

One factor is that employers today don't want just "employees"...they want "stars," stand-outs, the cream of the crop. It's essential, because in today's service-oriented, communications-dependent business climate, a company's success depends more than ever on the quality of the people it employs. That's why even in the midst of an economy with millions unemployed, good people are more in demand than ever—and more than ever they are writing their own tickets.

So what makes a star? It is not necessarily grade averages (although a 3.8 looks better than a 2.4 anytime). Most employers have had experience with eggheads who know the technical and theoretical aspects of their jobs inside and out, but lack the ability to apply their knowledge in a practical way, and are therefore ineffective. Besides, most professional-level jobs today are so specialized that there's no way a rookie could step in and be immediately proficient. Employers know that a certain learning curve is to be expected with any new employee. Therefore, if you can convince the employer that you are *capable of learning* the technical aspects of a new job, that's usually good enough.

Rarer than technical skills in young college graduates—and so much harder to teach—are *professional* skills. Professionalism is difficult to quantify, or even explain. Most employers feel toward professionalism the way retired Supreme Court Justice Potter Stewart felt toward pornography: "I know it when I see it." Whatever *it* is, if you are going to stand out in the job-hunting pack, employers are going to have to see it in you.

To project professionalism you have to strike the

perfect balance between enthusiasm and poise. You have to show that you are serious, open and steady, that you have a broad understanding of the field you intend to enter, that you want—and expect—to succeed, and that you have the personal power to be effective in a professional climate. If you can develop this professional style and master this professional mind-set, you will be the star everyone is looking for. There will be a thousand jobs out there with your name on them. In fact many companies will snatch you up whether they have an "opening" or not.

In business, the standard cliche for finding a job is "selling yourself." This doesn't mean that in order to get a job you have to sell your soul or sell your body (although these sometimes work too), but rather that you have to find an organization you think can help you, and convince the people in charge that you can help them.

Selling yourself is a good analogy, because getting a job involves the same mechanics that characterize any selling process. First you have to identify your market (the list of prospective employers), then you have to advertise (the resume), make the sales call (the interview), and negotiate the terms of the sale (salary, job description and working environment).

Then you have to sit down and take a deep breath. You just closed the biggest sale of your life—now you have to deliver.

The Prospects List

The first step in scoring the ultimate job is to develop a list of specific companies which fit your logistical and qualitative criteria. The logistical criteria include the company size, and the part of the country—or world—you want to live in. The qualitative criteria include the philosophy of the company, and similar "hidden" factors that are easily overlooked but can make a huge difference in your success. For instance, don't set your sights just on "large accounting firms in California." One could differ radically from another, particularly regarding treatment of entry-level people. Unless you look closely you won't be able to distinguish the fast track from the pit. Make it a point to find out about your prospective company's growth record, salary ranges for entry-level people, track record for promotions, and of course the current financial position (it's so much more fun to work for a company that is growing than one that is not).

While you're at it, make it a point to check out the caliber of the work your prospective employer puts out. This is very important. You don't have to look for the biggest company in the business, or the richest, but do seek out one that is committed to doing excellent work. If you join a company that is comfortable turning out shoddy or unimaginative work, you may become comfortable with shoddy or unimaginative work, too (after all, it *is* easier). And that, friends, is the Kiss of Death. Not only will it spoil your attitude, but it will compromise your record when you go to find another job. You may be able to "get by" doing mediocre work (a lot of people do)—and you may even get rich—but you will never be truly satisfied.

Think of your experience in college. Some of your professors demanded nothing short of excellence. You did better work for them. You studied harder, researched better, took more initiative, wrote and typed your papers more carefully. And you learned more and gained more satisfaction for it. This is the kind of environment you should look for in a job— particularly your first job, where your professional habits and standards are formed. Say what you will about the declining quality of goods and services in this country—the fact is excellence has never been more valued. Take care to develop and promote it.

There are several ways to research the background information you need on companies you are considering—sources ranging from industry directories to individual corporate financial reports. The library, of course, is a gold mine; just ask the librarian to help you find what you need. If your school has a career resources department, make sure you take advantage of it. Talk with people in your prospective employer's chamber of commerce. If possible, talk with people who work for the employer (just make sure you get more than one opinion) —or even those who work for "the competition."

Every salesperson has to spend time "qualifying the prospects." In this case, the time will be some of the most valuable you ever invest.

The Resume

The closest to perfection a person ever comes
is when he fills out a job application form.
—Stanley Randall

The two of us receive about ten resumes a week from people looking for work. Nine of them don't get more than a three-second glance. That's not unusual; most resumes are never read. Why? Because they are dull, poorly reproduced, too long, badly organized, out of date, and sometimes totally preposterous.

As we said before, a resume is an advertisement for you. And like every good advertisement, it must be constructed to gain attention, arouse interest and generate action. To do that effectively, a resume should contain the following elements: your statistical story, your photo, a phone number where you can be reached or left a message at all times, a brief description of who you *really* are—and a flair.

The statistical you. This is the objective part of your resume, where you list your educational history, work history, and vital statistics. It is the central element of any resume (unfortunately for most people it is the only element). There are many books which explain, in grueling detail, the various approaches to this objective self-presentation (we've listed a couple of the best in our reading list), so we won't belabor it here. However, we will give you one tip that most resume books seem to miss:

Quantify your work history. By this we mean describe it in objective terms. For example, if you worked as a salesperson for a department store throughout college you might write:

> **1977–81** Part-time salesperson (20 hrs/wk) in the men's clothing department at Macy's. Wrote annual sales of $74,000 year 1; $89,000 year 2; $116,000 year 3; and $131,000 year 4.

This sounds much more impressive than:

> **1977–81** Part-time salesperson, Macy's.

Instantly, prospective employers can see, in objective terms, the amount of responsibility you held, and measure the progress you made while on the job. Quantifying your work experience is the businesslike way to present your work history, and businesspeople respond to it.

But you say you've always had jobs that can't possibly be quantified this way. Think again. *All* jobs lend themselves to this type of conversion. Look at the following examples. Each is a typical college job one would not view as being terribly prestigious, but nonetheless is worthy of being quantified.

> **Cafeteria Cashier, Student Union.** Responsible for handling over 500 customers and $1,500 in cash every day.

> **Head Photographer, Sullivan Eagle (Sullivan College newspaper).** Responsible for scheduling and production of news, feature and sports photographs for weekly newspaper (average 25 photos per issue). Supervised staff of eight part-time student photographers.

> **Economics School Librarian.** Coordinated course material for 30 professors; oversaw lending library of over 200,000 volumes.

Get the point? No matter what job you've held, there is a way to describe and quantify it so a prospective employer immediately understands the amount of responsibility you carried. An added advantage to presenting your work experience quantitatively is that it invites comparison. While other candidates are submitting generic job descriptions and droning on about "coordinating the customer/company interface" (salesclerk), you will be making your case in clear, concise terms. Naturally, nine times out of ten you'll be the one who comes through looking like the best candidate.

Include your photo. Most resume counselors will tell you never to enclose a photo with your resume. Here's the conventional wisdom: a photo of a person evokes an emotional response. Therefore, if you enclose a photo you may prompt a negative emotional response in your potential employer...and why take chances?

But you are going to have to take that chance sooner or later anyway. Most interviewers decide within the first thirty seconds of the interview whether a candidate is suitable for the position. Why not get it over with? If it turns out that in the employer's mind you have "the right look," a photograph will *help* you get the interview. If you don't have "the right look," you would have been weeded out eventually anyway. Why waste your time?*

Okay, so your face would sink the Ninth Fleet. In that case a photograph may be even more valuable. Go to a professional photographer and ask him or her to capture your "best side." With the proper lighting and touchup, anyone can be made to look, uh...better. You have more of a chance of engineering that critical first impression with a good photograph than during the first tense thirty seconds of an interview.

On the other hand, you may be a virtual Thing of Beauty. In that case, not enclosing a photo could constitute a totally blown opportunity. Your resume may be a dud, but your glorious mug may get you the interview ...which in turn gets you the job.

---

*You didn't want to work for the rotten s.o.b. anyway.

Another advantage to enclosing a photograph is that hardly anyone else does it. All a personnel director usually has to go on is the typical stale, one- or two-page resume. And, as might be expected, most of these get "filed" immediately. By enclosing a picture, however, you add a new dimension to your resume and differentiate yourself. Plus, you lessen the likelihood of it being tossed (it's real tough to throw away someone's professionally-done photograph).

One final comment on pictures: always send a black and white, dull-finish photograph—never a full-color print. Black and white is considered more professional. Besides, it allows a photographer more latitude with lighting and touchup. The best size to send is 5″ by 7″ or wallet size.

The total you. Too many resumes deal exclusively with career and educational credentials. But in the professional world people hire people, not just "employees." And more often than not, the people who hire you will also have to work with you. You can bet they want to know more than just where you worked or attended school for the last umpteen years. Don't be afraid to let it be known who you are *outside* the work world— and this involves more than some contrived list of "hobbies." By revealing more of your personal side you further differentiate yourself, and may even hit a hot button with the person making the hiring decision.

One good way to present *the total you* on paper is to attach to your resume a one-page synopsis of your life. Written in a friendly, first-person tone of voice, the synopsis should reveal a good look at your personality, sense of humor and general philosophy. Specifics you could deal with in this "letter of introduction" include highlights of your background, personal interests, achievements and long-term objectives.

Don't view this as a brag sheet, but rather as a human interest story, like something you would find in the feature section of your Sunday paper. By letting your personality shine through, you will add the right dimension to round out the quantitative presentation of your work accomplishments.

Include a phone number. The dumbest mistake you can make in a resume is to fail to state where you can be reached or be left a message—at *all* times. It's amazing the number of job candidates with outstanding resumes who request that they not be called at their current job (a good idea, by the way), yet leave just their home phone number, which rings unanswered from nine to five. Don't make it a challenge for a prospective employer to contact you. *Always* include a phone number where you can be reached or be left a message during the workday.*

The unresume. Imagine a personnel director with thirty-five unread resumes in a stack on his desk. All have black type on white paper—except one. It's printed on yellow paper. Which one do you think will be read first? The one on the top of the pile? No way. The yellow one will, because it breaks the monotony of the stack of resumes. In fact, it will get more attention simply because it's different. Don't you want *your*

---

*Speaking of accessibility, an answering machine can be a great investment in both your professional and personal life. Try one. And don't concern yourself with regressives who "hate talking to those damn machines." Tell them it's not meant to take your place, just your messages.

resume to get that kind of attention? You bet.

If you're *really* creative you won't stop just at colored paper. You'll move into the major leagues of creative resume construction, with a true *Unresume:* a one-of-a-kind message directed to the specific industry, profession or company you want to break into. (A hidden benefit of the job-specific unresume is that it forces you to narrow down the type of work you want, not just what you'll take.)

We know of a young woman who wanted to land a job in the marketing division of a well-known wine company. To get the attention of the marketing department and show off her creative talent, she made her resume out of a wine bottle. The bottle was authentic, and the label was made to look authentic by presenting all her resume data in a type similar to that of the company's own label. As might have been expected, the marketing top brass were so impressed with her imaginative resume they offered her a position after only a short interview.

One graduate seeking a job as an accountant in a Big Eight accounting firm constructed his resume as a balance sheet. On the asset side he listed all his positive attributes, including a 3.6 GPA and a self-proclaimed dedication and willingness to work hard. On the liability side he presented the fact that he was fresh out of college, had little work experience and needed to be trained. In the equity section, he listed his achievements, awards and references. The concept was original and well executed. Best of all, it worked.

Another enterprising job-hunter targeted a job in computer sales. To demonstrate his in-depth understanding of computers, he presented his resume on computer paper in Fortran language.

A woman who wanted to join a publishing house demonstrated her originality by putting together a mock book as her resume. Chapter by chapter she presented all of the information a plain resume would have included. She titled her unresume *The Best Candidate.*

By the way, never forget the one word in a resume that could cost you an interview: the misspelled word. Of course, as Mark Twain once said, "It's a damn poor mind that can't think of more than one way to spell a word," but your resume isn't the place to demonstrate this talent. Proofread carefully. Don't let a misspelled word undermine the effectiveness of your resume and sabotage your chance for an interview.

Two wonderful examples of unresumes...ours. Jimmy wanted to get a job in advertising so he emulated one of the most successful ad campaigns of the late seventies, "The Dewar's Profile" for Dewar's scotch. His resume was an exact replica of the original format: same type style, "in-his-element" photograph, subheads and layout—right to the tee. Ad agencies loved it, because his unresume revealed a lot more about his capabilities than a traditional resume ever could. It showed he could not only identify a hot concept, but also handle all the logistical aspects of getting an ad produced from scratch. Chances are it stood out by a mile from all the "job summaries."

Jeff, also looking for a job in the advertising business, combined his resume with a portfolio of his writing samples into one piece. Using a simple photo album as the basis, he constructed a little story of his pre-professional life, starting with a poem he had written in the second grade, which his teacher had hung on the classroom wall: "My uncle has a little cow /

He milks it everyday / When I go to my uncle's house / I milk it then I play." From there he moved quickly (*very* quickly) to a narrated sampling of the articles and photographs he had had published in college. A single page at the end contained the educational and career logistics: the typical resume stuff. Jeff's idea was to take the scrapbook around in person to the agencies he wanted to work for. He was hired by the first company he showed it to.

One final comment on developing an unresume: whenever possible, it should be easily produced and not excessively expensive. This is not as important, however, if you are trying to land a job with one specific company. In this instance it's okay to get carried away, because you will need only one unresume...if it works.

Now more than ever you have to *sell* yourself on the job market when you get out of college. An unresume can be the perfect advertisement.

Going to Market

Once you've narrowed your list of prospective employers and have your resume (or unresume) together, your next step is to call each company and find out the name of the person responsible for hiring (make sure you get the correct spelling!). Then, call the person directly, introduce yourself, and say you will be sending your resume to his or her attention. That way, you will have the prospective employer looking for your resume, and it won't just become part of the pile of unsolicited mail that every executive has to deal with every day. It will receive greater respect and have a much stronger chance of being read.

Be sure to enclose a short cover letter informing the prospective employer that you will call within a week to make sure your resume was received. This is also a good place to restate your phone number.

After five working days, call each prospect who has not contacted you and follow through. Make a list of whom you've sent resumes to and whom you've called. This will save you the embarrassment of calling someone twice.

When you have a prospect on the phone, don't be afraid to assert yourself and ask to be interviewed. Restate your interest in the company and try to pin your contact down for an exact interview time. A good closing line is "Will Wednesday the twenty-sixth work for you? Morning or afternoon?" It may be one of the oldest closing lines in the book, but it works.

When you get the interview, always follow up by sending a short letter thanking the employer and confirming the time and location. This is important because it impresses the potential employer that you are taking the interview seriously and mean business. It also shows your professionalism and attention to detail. If nothing else, it gets your name in his or her mind one more time.

Face to Face: The Interview

While waiting in the reception room, the pre-interview jitters set in. You can't stop clearing your throat and glancing at your watch. Nervously, you fold and unfold your arms. You rub your sweaty palms into the cloth on your thighs and feel your clothing lose its crispness. With uneasy casualness, you force a smile at the receptionist who continues to glance—

or, if you're truly doomed, glare—at you. Impulsively, you pick up but immediately replace a magazine from the coffee table. You simply cannot concentrate on anything else but The Interview.

It probably shouldn't be like this, but it usually is. Most people become quivering fear-freaks at the thought of interviewing, because they put themselves under ridiculous pressure to put on a good show. Unfortunately, this self-imposed tension often produces the exact opposite effect. A candidate who is trying too hard—before the interview even gets started—usually comes off looking unprofessional and unsure.

No executive enjoys interviewing a bundle of nerves; an interviewer much prefers a candidate who appears relaxed and in control. Remember, an interviewer decides within thirty seconds whether you are suitable for the job. If you walk into the interview visibly uptight, you may be eliminated as a contender instantly. At that point, "going through the motions" becomes a real drag for the interviewer. Ideally, you want to peak and be at your best during the initial thirty seconds of the interview. If you sense you've made a good first impression, you will have the confidence for the rest of the interview.

Obviously, this is easier said than done. But it can be done, and you can do it if you follow a few basic guidelines.

Practice makes better. It sounds corny, but the best way to polish your interview persona and get your nervousness under control is to practice. *A lot.* Rehearse with a friend or roommate, in front of a mirror (try this and you'll be astonished at what you learn about how you come across to others), or by scheduling extra interviews just for the practice. Each time you talk about your work history, strengths, interests, etc., you'll sharpen your performance. Practicing takes time— and discipline—but it will give you that fine edge you can use your first time out.

Pre-guess questions. Analyze the nature of your interview and anticipate what you may be asked. To help you out, we've listed eighteen tough questions you would do well to practice answering. They are reprinted directly from the book, *One On One: Winning The Hiring Decision* by Theodore Pettus, which is the most practical, results-oriented handbook we've read on how to get a job. We recommend it (see our reading list).

1. Why should I hire you?
2. Why do you want to work here?
3. What causes you to lose your temper?
4. Who has had the greatest influence on you?
5. How long will you stay with the company?
6. What are your greatest accomplishments?
7. Do you have plans to continue your studies?
8. How do you feel about a male/female boss?
9. What would you like to be doing five years from now?
10. Why do you want to enter this particular field?
11. What honors have you earned?
12. What is your primary interest? Money, power, prestige, etc.?
13. How would a friend who knows you well describe you?
14. What courses did you like best?

15. What school activities did you participate in?
16. What books have you read in the last month? Movies? Plays?
17. How would you describe success?
18. How long will it take you to make a contribution to this company?

Before your first interview, formulate your response to these questions and practice delivering them in a dress rehearsal session. If you have difficulty, refer to the section in *One On One* where the author provides some good all-purpose, canned responses.

Pre-think your objectives. Before arriving for an interview, it's essential that you determine what you want from the job. What entrance-level salary will you accept? What benefits are essential? While it pays to remain flexible, don't get caught off guard and settle for something you will regret.

Look your best. The proper interview "look" depends on the job you are after. If you are interviewing with a bank you want to dress differently than if you are interviewing with a commercial art studio. Make it a point to investigate the image the company is trying to portray.

When in doubt, however, dress conservatively. The interview is a place to look serious, professional and well-groomed—like a leader. Men, wear a dark suit, white shirt, cranberry tie and beach sandals. Women, you too: wear a dark suit, open white shirt, teased hair and fluorescent red lipstick.* A good rule of thumb

---

*Just making sure you're awake.

is to avoid the latest fashions and quirky, personal styles. As Lawrence D. Schwimmer, creator of "Executives On The Fast Track" and other professional training programs, says, "In the Easter Bunny world you can wear anything you want and everyone will still love you. But in the business world, if you want to be taken seriously, you must dress with authority and present the corporate image."

Do your homework. You should have done this already: learn about the company with which you are interviewing, have a good sense of what they do and how they do it. Nobody who expects to be among "the chosen" flies by the seat of the pants anymore. Spend some time in the library reading articles, annual reports, and whatever information is available on the company you've scheduled an interview with. Take notes. And don't hesitate to drop a fact or statistic during the interview to demonstrate your knowledge. That will set you far above the rest of the candidates who haven't done their homework.

Articulate and be specific. Don't ramble, don't hedge and don't talk grandiose nonsense. Use facts and figures to make your points. In describing a previous job, talk in terms of your measurable accomplishments. Don't rely too heavily on emotion and dramatics. A bright interviewer will see right through them.

Smile and be friendly. Don't get carried away with the "momentous-ness" of the occasion by coming off as Mr. Intense or Ms. Serious. Let the interviewer see you are at ease, and not obsessed with making the right impression. Laugh occasionally and let yourself enjoy the conversation. A warm smile is a great ice-breaker.

Don't come on too strong. Too much friendliness can be worse than not enough...as can too much agreeability, enthusiasm and flattery. It's easy to come across as a sycophant if you try too hard to be what it is you think your interviewer wants you to be.

Be confident. That's the name of the game. Everything you say or do in the interview should contribute to creating an image of confidence and self-assurance. Why is confidence a key factor? Because everyone wants to pick a winner, and winners have lots of confidence.

But be careful not to overplay your confidence. Don't appear to know more than, or talk down to, your interviewer—it's too easy for him or her to get even. Remember, this person decides whether you are hired or sent a "thanks anyway" letter.

Let 'em talk. If the interviewer does a lot of talking, that's good. It usually means he or she is definitely interested in you, and wants to give you the most information and best possible impression of the company. Sometimes, however, it merely means he or she likes to talk at a captive audience. Either way, be a good listener by maintaining eye contact and concentrating on what the interviewer is saying. Don't interrupt or become impatient. There will be plenty of time for you to blow your horn later on.

Ask for the salary range. This is a good way to qualify your prospective employer. It allows you to compare the salary with other offers you may have already received, and with your own pre-established objectives. Perhaps the biggest value, however, is in using the information to get the best deal. If you know right away that the salary range is $14,000–$18,000, then you can come up with twenty great reasons why you deserve the maximum! Why start at $14,000 per year when you can start at $18,000?

When they make you an offer—shut up. The smartest thing to do when you are offered a low starting salary is keep quiet. If you let the interviewer grow uncomfortable with the silence, he or she will soon realize you aren't biting. You can even add to the impression by looking down and acting disappointed. He or she may increase the offer. Be warned, it will be just as uncomfortable for you. But if you want more money and think you can get it, let the silence become impenetrable. If you're pushed for an answer, just say, "I'm thinking it over." Keep in mind that the silent treatment requires skill and it *can* backfire. Use your judgment.

Be in demand. Subtly, let your prospective employer know that you are "talking" with his competitors. You don't want to come across as a wise guy, yet it doesn't hurt to let the employer know that he or she is not the only game in town. You might drop a line like "Yes, that's the same kind of insurance plan that Brewster Associates offered me." This will help establish your worth in the eyes of the interviewer.

Persistence pays. If you want a job badly enough, keep knocking on the door. Eventually, it may open. If a company you had high hopes of working for rejects you, it's not necessarily the final scene. In fact, getting turned down may be your best opportunity. From the point of initial rejection, you can try all types of creative approaches to demonstrate your talents and skills. Write follow-up letters, interview in another division, or get in touch with other key people in the organization. Do whatever it takes to get them to recognize and appreciate your potential value. But don't be a pest. Once you come to the conclusion that nothing is going to work out, cut your losses and focus your energy elsewhere.

Imagination can do it. Suppose you're absolutely sure you've found the job of your dreams. The only problem is that fifteen other candidates, just as qualified as you, want the position just as much. When you find yourself in this predicament, it's time to break out of the traditional job-search mode and do something outrageous. Not foolish, but outrageous. You must show the potential employer why he or she should pick you out of the crowd. You must differentiate yourself from the others with some sort of unexpected gambit that impresses the hell out of the hiring decision-maker.

One such ingenious ploy was related to us by a friend of ours, Kent. Kent recalls having to hire a new sales representative and having difficulty making a final selection. Each candidate was very qualified, but no one really stood out. That all changed, however, when Kent returned from a business luncheon one afternoon and found a large manila envelope on his desk. In it were two things: a fork and a handwritten message which read, "I want this job so bad I can taste it." Needless to say, Kent was so impressed with the applicant's imaginative and somewhat brazen follow-up that he ended *his* search with that person.

Rejecting rejection. Ouch! Nobody likes to be rejected. But at some point it's going to happen, and if you're prepared, you can maintain the momentum of your job search by handling it maturely and creatively.

When you hear the interviewer say, "We've decided to continue our search, thanks anyway," accept the decision graciously. Do not act hurt (and please, do not tell the interviewer to take the job and shove it). Instead, while the interviewer's sympathies are on your side, use that emotional climate to gather valuable information that will put your job search back on track. Ask the interviewer where you blew it (if you received a rejection letter, call the interviewer as soon as possible), what you said or did wrong, what you lacked in terms of education or experience...find out just why you didn't fit the bill. Or try a reversal technique: ask the interviewer what he or she would have done differently if he or she were in your shoes. The answers to these questions will help you grow professionally and better prepare you for your next interview.

It's also a good idea to ask the interviewer if he or she knows of any other employment opportunities in the field. It's a long shot, but worth asking. You may get a hot lead.

As we've said, to succeed in the interview, you want to do your homework and be ready; look your best and talk your best; ask the right questions and give the right answers; and, most of all, deliver a confident, professional image. Doing all these things will give you the competitive edge in the interview arena. But what, if with all that, you still can't get the job you want?

The Hustle

Well, what if? Suppose the field you decided to

enter is dying...or your Unresume and creative interviewing style found no audience...or you were beat
out fair and square. Statistically speaking, some of
you will suffer this fate.

It's not the end of the world. In fact, it may be the
beginning of your career. Think about it: if you managed to make it through the long years of college, you
must have something of value to sell to society (aside
from the gold in your class ring). It may not be directly
related to your major, or the job you had your heart
set on, but it may very well make you a lot of money.

We're talking about ad hoc entrepreneurship—
sometimes known as *the hustle*. Open your mind to
it. Maybe you could start a commercial cleaning
service, a T-shirt silk-screening business, a lunch truck
serving local factories. There are literally hundreds
of needs in any community that a hardworking, enterprising young person like yourself can fill for a fee.

The hustle is more in style today than it has ever
been, and there are quite a few books available that
can help you get started, even if you have no experience or money (we've listed our favorites in our
reading list). In the meantime, we'll give you what we
feel are the two most important principles of the
hustle: 1) be the best at what you do; and 2) be the
organizer, subcontracting as much actual labor as
possible.

Once you get started, you may find, as countless
people have, that entrepreneurship is what you were
after all along. Jimmy's friend, Marissa, a commercial art graduate from UCLA, decided to strike out
on her own after several months of not finding a
suitable job in Los Angeles. She printed up some
business cards, put together a portfolio and started

soliciting local businesses for work as a free-lance photographer (she had been the top photographer for the *UCLA Bruin*). A year later, she's established a regular clientele, good contacts and a growing income. "I still have my eyes open for the ultimate ad agency job," she says, "but to tell the truth, it's going to have to be pretty perfect to take me away from this."

Don't be surprised if your hustle turns into a successful, long-term enterprise. Being entrepreneurs ourselves, we welcome you to a high-spirited community.

Body Snatchers, Head-Hunters and Flesh Peddlers

They are also known as personnel agencies and executive search firms. And although you probably won't use them your first time out, they are valuable and you should know about them for future reference.

There are two types of placement agencies: one that works for the company and one that works for the job applicant. A private employment or personnel agency works exclusively for a candidate by locating a company with an appropriate job opening. An executive search firm works on behalf of a client company by trying to fill a position with the best possible candidate. Private employment agencies usually specialize in basic skills jobs such as secretary, data entry person or bookkeeper. Search firms, or "body snatchers", on the other hand, concentrate on middle or upper management level positions. With an employment agency, the applicant usually pays the placement fee; with a search firm, the client company always foots the bill. It's important to note that you actually *retain* a private employment agency to find you a job, whereas you merely make yourself known to a search firm...they may later invite you for an interview with one of the client companies.

So why conduct a job search yourself? Why bother with "creative" resumes and interviews? Why not sit back and let a placement agency line up lots of interviews with lots of companies? Sooner or later, a job offer is bound to come along, right? Well, maybe someday it will work that way for you, but not your first time out of the gate. Here's why: executive search firms rarely place anyone making less than $35,000 a year (and unless you developed a perpetual-motion machine in your science lab, that salary's going to be out of your league). They are paid solely by their client companies to locate the best possible candidate for a specific position. From each placement, they receive a percentage of the first year's salary—usually 12% or more. If the candidate works out, they get more orders. As a result, search firms make it a point to thoroughly check out a candidate's background and experience before they recommend him or her. As a fresh graduate, you have very little of either, so they probably won't be inclined to risk their reputation on you.

Private employment agencies, on the other hand, are typically small mom-and-pop companies that often double as temporary-help agencies. Since employment agencies work exclusively on behalf of the job applicant, you may be tempted to give them all the responsibility for finding your first job. But employment agencies are usually understaffed. Worse, they are distracted from their function of finding permanent job placements because they are forced to spend an inordinate amount of time collecting fees from previously-placed job applicants. (It seems like everybody tries to forget about paying an employment agency.) Furthermore, they only hear about job openings from the newspaper or from companies where they have placed a temporary worker. They just don't deal in the big leagues. The final reason we don't recommend them initially is because they can't get you a job. They can only get you an interview. Getting hired—the hard part—is all up to you. Why give up a substantial part of a starting salary for a connection you should be able to make on your own?

Search Firms Are Good Later On

After you're earning over $35,000 a year, executive search firms can be an ideal source of job opening information. Here's why you should use them almost exclusively after having gained experience and expertise in your field.

Secrecy. If, while job-hunting, you blindly send your resume in response to newspaper or magazine classified ads that cite no company name, your resume just may land in your own company's hands! (Some firms place ads just to see who among their employees is "looking around.") That's like sending a telegram to the president of your company stating that you're no longer committed to the organization. If you hook up with a search firm, however, you're guaranteed privacy as well as an inside look at what attractive positions are open.

Time. No one making $35,000 a year should be spending time pounding the pavement on Job Search

Avenue. By having someone else be your eyes and ears, you can better utilize your time.

The iceberg rule. Only 20% of an iceberg lies above the water; the other 80% remains below the surface, hidden from view. Likewise, only 20% of all job openings are advertised. The other 80% remain confidential and unknown to the public. Guess who's tipped off to the 80%? You guessed it: the executive search firms. By aligning yourself with these specialists, you increase your exposure in the job market by 400%.

The company pays. When a search firm successfully places you, your new employer pays the commission. On a placement of $50,000, that could be as high as $25,000, depending on the fee structure.

Someday search firms may be able to help you immeasurably. As many professionals have discovered, changing jobs can be the quickest and surest road to success.

6: The Mental Shakedown Cruise

This is one cruise where you *want* to lose your baggage.

Based on the messages you've received all your life—from your parents, teachers, friends, the mass media and your environment in general—you've developed certain attitudes about yourself and how you fit into the world (this is what philosophy professors refer to as your "world view"). If you're like most people raised in this accelerative, sometimes neurotic society, it makes sense that many of your attitudes are out of date. Others are probably downright destructive.

Lots of otherwise competent people sabotage their chances for success and enjoyment as professionals because of certain hang-ups. Don't let that happen to you. Life in the Real World may turn out to be a lot simpler than you think, provided you don't over-complicate it. And it may turn out to be a lot of fun, if you allow it to be.

Now that you are about to move into a new era of your life, clean the slate. Step back and evaluate your world view, attitude by attitude, to see which aspects are worth keeping and which should go. It's a good time to go on a *mental shakedown cruise.*

We recommend the following seven steps on the mental shakedown cruise. Undoubtedly, there are others that you will be able to find on your own.

Step 1: Read Your Labels

You were always losing your toys as a kid. You could never find your socks. The people around you were happy to supply a name for your problem: you were *forgetful.*

Over the years forgetful became something of a joke ("Johnny would forget his head if it wasn't attached"), your little quirk, a handy and harmless conversation piece. But now, many years later, the prophecy has fulfilled itself. You are truly forgetful. In fact, it has become a comfortable and protected part of your identity, a little friend you can run to and hide behind when the going gets rough.

But being forgetful is not going to cut it in the circles to which you aspire. Try it and see. The first time your boss asks you to explain a missed deadline, knock yourself lightly on the head (a la "I coulda-hada V-8") and say, "Oh, isn't that just like me! I'd forget my head if it wasn't attached!" You'll see what we mean.

Forgetful is just one of the many labels people hang on themselves. Think about it: what are the labels you have hanging on you? A good way to identify them is to listen to the ways you describe yourself to other people:

"I work best under pressure."

"I spend money the minute I get my hands on it."
"I just can't speak in front of large groups."
"I'm always late for everything."
"I can't resist chocolate."
"I guess I'm just not the brainy type."
...And on and on.

Do you really want to go through life pegged with limitations like these? Shuck them off! If you're forgetful, get organized. Don't permit yourself to forget things. The skills of organization are not something you were born with; like all skills they are learned, and must be practiced to be mastered. You can get started with some organizational skills you'll learn in the following sections of this book. Beyond that, you can talk to people who are well organized, or read one of the many books on the subject.

Changing bad organizational habits, money habits, work habits, eating habits or habits of any kind can be tough. But the toughest part is changing your attitude. One of the most exciting realizations you will ever have is that you *can* change your behavior, and thereby change your life. It may even turn you into a self-improvement junkie. And why not? It's a great addiction.

So read your labels and decide whether they represent truth in packaging. You're going to run into plenty of problems as it is...don't add to them with self-fulfilling and self-imposed limitations. Give yourself every chance to be all you can be.

Step 2: Break the Rules

Say you are looking through the "positions available" section of a trade magazine in your field.

You read an ad describing the perfect job for you, just the job you've been looking for. The ad specifies your exact capabilities, the money's right, and the company has a good reputation. Just as you are getting excited you spot the catch: the job requires at least three years' experience. "Oh well," you console yourself, "I guess I have to pay some dues before I can have a job like that."

Don't give up so easily! Consider the situation more closely. Employers are looking for the best employees they can find. And in order to limit the time it takes to find the best person, they limit their options to the group most likely to fit the bill: the experienced group.

But employers care more about whether a person is right for the job than whether he or she fits some sort of convenient demographic. If you really believe you are the perfect candidate, and can communicate it, the employer will be glad to talk with you. If you can prove it, you'll be hired.

Yet, most people would take the ad at its word and move on to the next listing without much thought. That's because we have been raised in a society that very much values the concept of following the rules. Following the rules and recognizing authority (the printed word being one of the most authoritative authorities of all) have been critical to the functioning of our standardized, synchronized society...and most of us have had at least sixteen good years of training and practice. As Alvin Toffler wrote in *The Third Wave:*

> Built on the factory model, mass education
> taught basic reading, writing and arithmetic, a bit

of history and other subjects. This was the "overt curriculum." But beneath it lay an invisible or "covert curriculum" that was far more basic. It consisted—and still does in most industrialized societies—of three courses: one in punctuality, one in obedience, and one in rote-repetitive work.

But in these ways mass education has prepared us for a world that has since changed. The Real World is no longer structured as a grid or linear flow chart, but as a network. In other words, there are a lot of different routes that can get you where you want to be, when you want to be there. So next time you run into a roadblock, go around it.

This does not mean that you will not occasionally run into vestiges of hard, fast rules in the professional world. You will, but chances are the rules no longer apply—there are simply too many exceptions. The trick is to know when *you* are the exception. That's why re-evaluating your relationship with rules, structure and convention is one of the most critical shakedown cruises of all.

Step 3: Life is Unfair

Jimmy Carter, in a nationally televised press conference, answered a reporter's charge of inequity in government social policy by saying, "Life is unfair."

That statement caused quite a furor, and political pundits point to it as a giant step in Jimmy Carter's political demise. Maybe so, but it was also the most profound thing to ever come out of the man's mouth.

Life *is* unfair. That's tough to accept, because we have been steeped in the notion that as enlightened people living in an enlightened society, we are somehow protected from injustice. But we're not. Certainly we all have more control over our lives than we often think. Yet there is a level on which we have no control, and on this level there is still a lot of senseless, random pain and injustice flying around. It makes sense that from time to time some of it is going to hit us. There's nothing we did to invite it, and there's nothing we can do to stop it.

Life in general—and professional life in particular—demands a certain amount of equanimity. Get in touch with your sense of self that is independent of the day-to-day ups and downs. Don't waste time gnashing your teeth and shaking your fists over that which you have no control. Forget about luck. Forget about what you think life ought to be and accept it for the exciting and unpredictable affair it is.

Step 4: The Problem with Problems

The surest way to be plagued by problems is to try to eliminate them from your life. It's called the *everything-is-going-to-smooth-out trap.*

As Jeff recalls: "I used to spend a lot of time in college daydreaming about life after graduation. I saw myself in my neat apartment with my awesome stereo system, hot tub, waterbed, and futuristic electronic alarm clock which would alert me every morning to the start of a brand-new day, at which time I would take a zesty shower and head off in my sports car, looking and feeling like a million bucks, to my stimulating professional job, where I would work with other Young Creative People on all kinds of exciting projects, and after which I would eat a light dinner and head off to a small, funky club where I would play my guitar and during breaks join my latest heartthrob and a small group of good friends for a drink."

That's dreamland.

Jeff goes on, "It turns out that I've got the nice home and great career, and in some ways things are better for me than I expected. But my life doesn't even remotely resemble that carefree and exciting vision I used to dream about. Many mornings when my futuristic electronic alarm clock alerts me to the start of a brand-new day, my first thought is of a problem. I'm behind schedule on a project; the photos I received from the lab are fuzzy; I'm having a conflict with one of my clients...the problems seem to never end."

And they never will. Sometimes they are more plentiful or more difficult than at other times. Sometimes we have no control over them and sometimes they are clearly our fault. But we will always have them.

That's the trouble with the Real World: it's full of problems. Many people feel that the very appearance of a problem calls their competence into question, which immediately undermines their confidence. But that reaction is eliminated the minute you understand that life's problems come with the territory. They do not develop because you are bad person and deserve to be punished, but rather because you are a human being on the planet Earth. This is an important point, because facing a problem demands that your confidence level be at its highest. So try this: the next time you run into a problem, look at it as a challenge. Expand with excitement and confidence. Stand up to it. Stare it down. Tear it up and devour it. If we sound like your junior high basketball coach, it's because to deal with problems effectively, you really do have to accept them as wholesome challenges, and consciously and deliberately psyche yourself up.

Step 5: What's Right with Being Wrong

The best way to deal with mistakes and failures, as with problems, is to change your attitude about them. Mistakes do not happen because you are incompetent (some do; you're not getting off the hook *that* easily). They are an unavoidable result of taking action. Every course of action involves risk—which involves the distinct possibility of failure. Consequently you are going to be wrong a certain percentage of the time. But wrong isn't necessarily bad, and that one simple fact sheds a whole new light on the matter.

As Donald and Elenore Laird wrote in their book *The Art of Getting Things Done:*

> Next to being right, the best of all things is to be clearly and definitely wrong, because you will come out somewhere. If you go buzzing about between right and wrong, vibrating and fluctuating, you come out nowhere; but if you are absolutely and thoroughly wrong, you have the good fortune of knocking against the facts that set you straight again.

Granted, it is difficult to take comfort in this kind of attitude when you've just screwed something up beyond all recognition, and everyone knows it. That's the bad thing about mistakes and failures: they hurt... sometimes they hurt other people. The good thing about mistakes and failures is that you can learn from them.

So go a little easier on yourself next time you blow it. Look at the situation objectively. Find out what went wrong. Did you fail because you tried to do more than you were capable of? That's a common beginner's mistake; next time be more realistic. Did a mistake slip through because you didn't double-check your work? Make double-checking an ironclad rule. Did you miss a deadline because you underestimated the amount of time your task would require? Next time plan your work more carefully.

Jimmy has developed an interesting exercise for capitalizing on his failures. On top of a yellow legal pad he writes the words *What did I learn?* Then he lists every mistake he made that led to his failure, and every lesson learned from it. After getting it all on paper he puts it in his "lessons learned" file, which he refers to every time he needs to remind himself that he's smarter than he used to be. The "what-did-I-learn?" exercise is a good confidence-builder that will help you face failure and grow from it.

Step 6: Practical Perfectionism

There's something to be said for people who care enough to always do their best. And it's usually said with raises, bonuses, perks and accolades. If you're someone who strives for perfection, congratulations; you're already miles ahead of your peers. If you're someone who expects to achieve it, however, you're on the wrong track entirely.

There are two distinct approaches to excellence in the professional world: *practical perfectionism* and *neurotic perfectionism* (can you guess which one is better?). Neurotic perfectionists feel they need to be the best at everything they do. In order to succeed, they have to somehow further the state-of-the-art on every project. This unreasonable, idealized expectation makes progress tortuously slow. ("It's not quite right yet. I'll have to come back and work on it some more later.") Finishing something is almost impossible. ("It still needs more work.") As a result, the anxiety level of the neurotic perfectionist is high, and productivity is low. Nine times out of ten their misdirected masterpiece, finished under deadline duress, is worth a lot less than a "perfectly adequate" approach would have been.

Practical perfectionism, on the other hand, means commitment to excellence, attention to detail, and systematic, results-oriented work habits. It also means knowing when to quit. Often as much energy is required to take a project the last 10% in quality as it required to take it the first 90%. You have to ask yourself if it's worth it. Sometimes it is and sometimes it isn't. A business letter, for instance, is generally meant to communicate information. A first draft most often suffices—just get your points on paper and send them off. When debating the benefits of a higher degree of quality, in any endeavor, be sure you consider the energy required to achieve it. Look at it this way: when you get one thing done you've created the space to do another thing.

Allow us to hedge on one aspect of our argument. In the first year or two of your career it is a good idea, if you must err, to err on the side of "too perfect." Considering the work quality level of most new graduates, it will definitely make people take notice. It is much better to learn your professional skills too well than to not learn them well enough.

Step 7: Fraud-Guilt

*True success is overcoming the fear of
becoming successful.*

—Paul Sweeny

People who become particularly successful often suffer from what we call *fraud-guilt*. You experience fraud-guilt when you believe you do not deserve what you've managed to achieve. You may feel that your success is all the result of a fluke, or because you were particularly adept at fooling people. As a result, you live in fear that someone is going to find out the truth and expose you to the world. Worse yet, you suspect, down in the secret recesses of your heart, that the world already knows you are a fraud, and everyone is keeping it under wraps out of some sort of unspoken conspiracy of good taste.

There are four typical symptoms of fraud-guilt:

1. You stay in the background, away from the action, hiding lest someone should spot you for what you really are.

2. You shy away from conflict, fearful that you might anger people sufficiently to make them lose their tempers and expose you for what you really are.

3. You avoid making decisions because you fear you'll make a wrong one and everyone will see you for what you really are.

4. Since your fundamental incompetence can't help but sometimes show through, you are haunted by mistakes and problems...and you spend most of your time putting out fires and plugging the holes in the dike rather than making things happen.

There are two cures for fraud-guilt. One involves twelve years with a psychiatrist. The other, in our opinion far easier and possibly even more effective, is to look around you and see what a jerk everyone else is. We're serious. There's no quicker confidence-builder than the realization that you're not the only one who thinks he or she's got something to hide, and that everybody must deal with the ghosts of insecurity and self-doubt. (Well, almost everybody. There are a few fascinating exceptions—you'll know them when you meet them.)

7: Managing Yourself

Does the president of Exxon work a thousand times harder than you do? Of course not, but the results of his actions are a thousand times greater.

The classic American concept of "the more you sweat, the more you get" may have held a glimmer of truth back in the days when people grew what they ate. Today, however, it is meaningless. In fact, the supersuccessful almost never work as hard as the merely successful. They work smarter.

Whatever you do as a professional, it will involve managing resources. The most important of these resources is yourself. Managing yourself as a professional is an active exercise. It is something to be looked upon coolly and objectively: "Okay, what I've got here in front of me is a certain amount of intelligence, energy, and skills. Now, how can I get the most out of them?"

The concept of "managing yourself" may seem to have a workaholic or neurotic edge. Actually, the opposite is true; workaholics and neurotics are notoriously bad self-managers. Good self-management

means working *fewer* hours, because you are getting
more done in less time. It also means gaining a good
understanding of your limitations and potential, and
determining the role you want work to play in your
life, thus freeing yourself from the anxiety of dealing
with cross-purposes and unrealistic, self-imposed
demands.

Self-management is an idea that will become
increasingly important in the professional world as
the pressure for efficiency grows,* stakes are raised,
and competition gets hotter.

It seems to be an obsession of professionals to
search for ways to make themselves more productive.
Today an entire "professional development" industry
has come about in response to this need, churning out
hundreds of books, seminars, cassettes, articles and
studies every year. As a result, there are well-defined
bodies of knowledge on a variety of self-management
concepts, including stress management, time management, decision making, problem solving and personal
motivation.

Your authors had a client who is one of the most
successful "professional developers" in the country,
a consultant and lecturer on everything from assertiveness to sales technique to self-presentation. As she
says of that long list of concepts: "It's all the same
stuff."

---

*There is a lot of room for efficiency improvement. A 1981 study
reported in the *Wall Street Journal* shows that the typical white-collar
worker is productive only four hours a day. That's sure to surprise
those of you who thought the workaday world was a high-pressure
grind. If you worked hard in school, you may be better off than
you thought.

And it is. Ultimately, self-management boils down to "a job worth doing is worth doing well," "a stitch in time saves nine," and "a bird in hand is worth two in the bush."

Old ideas perhaps, but important ideas nevertheless ...trite because they're true. For the young professional, good self-management skills cannot be overemphasized; take the time to learn and master them. Following are highlights of self-management methods that have been tested and approved by millions of professionals, including us. They consist of pretty equal amounts of attitude and technique. Most of the methods are not original, but the result of years of trial and error in practical use. For a more in-depth look at the important area of self-management, see the reading list.

The PIE Model

The PIE (Plan, Implement, Evaluate) model is one of the most powerful self-management forces you will ever tap into.

One reason some people work hard and still fail is that they concentrate a disproportionate amount of effort on the implementation—the actual doing— of a project, while neglecting planning and evaluation, which are just as important for achieving long-term success.

Each stage of the PIE model is simple in principle. In the planning stage you project, forecast, brainstorm the "what ifs," and formulate your strategy for accomplishment. Good planning is one of the most cost-effective uses of professional time and energy. Yet, ironically, some people try to justify their bad planning or lack of planning with the excuse that they didn't have enough time. But when you know what your goal is on a project, and what steps, in what order, you intend to take to achieve your goal, you are less likely to make time-consuming false starts and wrong turns. In that way good planning always saves more time than it takes. There is another advantage to good planning, one that relates more to attitude than work. When you plan a project effectively, you are saved the anxiety of never knowing what your next step is going to be, or how far along you are, or even when you're done.

Evaluation is likewise an extremely cost-effective investment of time and energy. In the evaluation stage you examine the outcome of your planning and implementation of a project to determine what went wrong, what went right, and why. This final analysis is an invaluable opportunity to improve. While a project is still fresh in your mind is a great time to look back and see how a similar project could be handled better in the future. It's even a good idea in some cases to actually write up a project critique and save it for future reference.

The temptation, however, is to get caught up in the implementation of a project and focus a disproportionate amount of your effort and time on it. Everyone sees the value of implementation; after all, that's when the project actually happens. It's not nearly as exciting to work through the nebulous planning stage or to spend time sorting out what happened after all is said and done.

But, even though implementation is the favored

stage, it's not always handled very well. Professionals often have one big problem with implementation: they stop before they're finished. In their own defense these people will tell you that they look only at the big picture and don't concern themselves with the piddly details. This myth about professionals dealing exclusively with the big picture is perpetuated because it is a great cop-out for laziness and lack of discipline. People who aren't good at details usually aren't so hot at the big picture, either. It's true that as you rise to higher positions in the professional world, you will deal with problems at a higher level of implementation. You will supervise other implementors rather than deal with the actual work directly. But no matter how high you go, you will never be freed from details. There are just some situations and problems that have to be looked at closely and in their entirety—by you. President Reagan, for instance, is known for not getting involved in the minutiae of government programs. Yet is is not unusual for him to isolate himself for hours at a time to work on the nuances of a speech.

Just as pennies make dollars, details make accomplishments. Without follow-through on details, you're inviting needless problems and complications to occur that will undermine the results you are trying to achieve. Although good follow-through may never be noticed, bad follow-through is almost always noticed. Whatever you let fall through the cracks will be laying there waiting to trip you later on.

The PIE Model—Plan, Implement, Evaluate—is one of the truly fundamental principles of professional success. Try it on your next project...job-hunting, for instance.

Get Organized

Being a professional means being organized, efficient and reliable. Excuses such as "it slipped my mind" or "I ran out of time" are not acceptable in the Real World. (When was the last time you heard of a doctor "spacing out" surgery?)

Organization is a relatively simple task. Basically, it can be reduced to the following two principles.

1. Organize your tools. By tools we mean whatever it takes to get the job done, anything from a wrench to a tax schedule. If you don't have them, get them. If you can't get them, then you should consider that maybe you are not equipped to do the job after all. This is an important point. If you can train yourself to recognize an impossible job in its earliest stages, you will save yourself a huge amount of time, energy, and frustration.

2. Organize your workspace. Find a place where you can be comfortable. Discomfort is an annoying distraction (it can also be a source of self-pity, something you don't need when you're already pitying yourself for having to work in the first place). Keep in mind that a desk is not a place to stack items you want to remember. Your desk is one of your most important organization elements. It's a tool to expedite the receiving and processing of information. Have only one project on your desk at one time and get rid of the things you're not ready to deal with.

The Screaming Yellow Grid

To be truly organized as a professional you must approach your work systematically, and that means subscribing to a *system* of personal organization. With such a system, you will be the person who never forgets an appointment, deadline, birthday, or occasion. You will be more confident, collected, and in control.

In order for your personal organization system to work, however, it has to fit your needs exactly. You must be comfortable with it, and see its benefits every time you use it. If you have the slightest doubt about your system, you won't use it to its potential (or use it at all). Choose carefully. There are a lot of systems out there, some of which are so complicated and cumbersome they actually consume more time than they save. Others are designed narrowly for one profession.

Over the past several years, Jimmy has developed his own system for personal productivity. He has used it religiously, continually refining it in the process. The system consists of two basic components: a Shaeffer-Eaton Month-at-a-Glance appointment book (okay, Shaeffer-Eaton, pay up) and an 8½-by-11-inch sheet of yellow paper that you transform into the Screaming Yellow Grid (named after the famous Zonkers) by marking it like the sample on pages 126 and 127.

The Month-at-a-Glance calendar records long-term appointments, plans, and occasions; those that occur at least seven days into the future, beyond the scope of your grid. (A hidden benefit of the calendar is that at the end of each year you can easily transfer all the birthdays and special occasions into your new calendar. They'll never slip your mind again!)

The yellow 8½-by-11-inch sheet, with its circles, dots, lines and boxes, is the key to the system. On it you fill in every appointment, meeting, project, phone call, or special occasion you want to remember within the next seven days. It then becomes your master schedule for the week. The yellow color will enable your grid to stand out—"scream"—from all the other forms, letters, and paperwork that inevitably cross your desk. You'll never wonder where it's hiding.

At the beginning of every week (or the end of the previous week), bring your Month-at-a-Glance calendar together with your Screaming Yellow Grid for a twenty- to thirty-minute planning session. You'll need at least this much time to gather and give sufficient consideration to everything you must (and want to) accomplish during the upcoming week. To gather your list of possible tasks, check three places:

1. The "next week" box on last week's grid, where you have written this week's phone calls, appointments and special projects that came to your attention last week (it's simpler than it sounds).

2. Your Month-at-a-Glance calendar, for appointments and special occasions scheduled previously.

3. Your in-basket or work-in-progress folder, for additional items you want to schedule time to work on this week.

After you have gathered all the items demanding your attention, evaluate them and schedule them for appropriate days on your new grid. List the items, placing phone calls above the dotted line, projects and assignments below the dotted line, and special occasions in the box. Fill in each day on the grid during this planning session.

To keep your schedule realistic, write next to each item the time you estimate it will take. And be reasonable; experts agree that one of the biggest

THE SCREAMING YELLOW GRID

○ MONDAY

○ WEDNESDAY

○ FRIDAY

○ SUNDAY

○ TUESDAY

○ THURSDAY

○ SATURDAY

NEXT WEEK

front

back

Here's an example of one day.

MONDAY ⑩   eye doctor appointment 2:45 pm

WEDNES

1 • Mark Lewis (Re: proofs) 423-9522
3 • Meg at LMI 212-743-1507
6 • T (Re: New Layouts) 443-7252
2 • Dan Damberg (Re: Colour Key for MPF Job) 802-864-0619
7 • Tim at Paladin (Re: List Promotion) 443-7250

---

10 • PCS Budget and Projection Due ⟨2 HRS.⟩
4 • Staff Meeting 11 AM ⟨45 MIN⟩
8 • List Research for Wheeler Communications ⟨1 HR.⟩
5 • Lunch w/ Mike Fitzpatrick 12:30 PM
9 • Review Hotel Contacts w/ Catherine ⟨30 MIN⟩

TUESDAY ⑪   Big Brothers Banquet 1 PM

THURSDAY

• Doug Whitaker (Re: Mail
• Michelle   Dates 573-16...

mistakes executives make is not allowing enough time to complete a task. Remember, you're the boss of your own time. Always allow enough of it to get things done, and don't jam a day with more projects and calls than you can reasonably accomplish. You'll only frustrate yourself.

Every morning when you arrive at work, take a few minutes to go over the items scheduled for that day, and rank them numerically according to their importance. This will save you the appreciable time (and anxiety) of making "what-should-I-do-next?" decisions all day long. Always schedule your high-priority/high-payoff items (which generally aren't so easy to do) before your low-priority/low-payoff items (which often just give the illusion of getting something done). This last point is a key element of almost any effective time-management system, and its power is amazing.

As you complete each item during the day, draw a line through it on your grid. This will keep you posted on what you've done and have left to do. Best of all, it gives you the great feeling of being able to proclaim a task totally and forever *done*.

At the end of each day, reschedule the items you did not complete for the next day or later in the week. If you've set your initial schedule wisely, this shouldn't happen too often.

While at work, keep your grid on or near your desk at all times. It will help you stay on track and enable you to schedule new things quickly. One good place to keep it is attached to the inside cover of your Month-at-a-Glance calendar; that will keep it from getting dog-eared. (That's also a great place to keep any papers you absolutely *have* to look at that day...you can't help but run into them.)

Other planning systems exist which may suit your needs too, but the Screaming Yellow Grid is flexible, practical, and time-proven. Give it a try!

One final note of warning about organization: Don't overdo it. It can be one of the most insidious means of procrastination there is, even more dangerous because it creates the illusion of getting something done. Organization is a *means* to productivity; by itself it produces nothing. Keep it in perspective.

Getting It Done

> *Hard work ain't easy.*
>
> —Joe Salzman

Discipline: it's the single biggest factor for success. There are three kinds of discipline: 1) personal discipline, the drive that keeps you moving toward your long-term, personal goals; 2) the day-to-day discipline that puts you on top of the ongoing details of your daily affairs; and 3) the special, bite-the-bullet discipline that gets you through particularly awful projects and trying times. Each is different and each is important.

The simple fact is that most people are lazy. There is a kind of fear associated with hard work. Growing up, most people learn to associate work with coercion (by parents and teachers) and deprivation of freedom and fun. Finally, as adults, it is inconceivable to many people that work could be anything but a necessary evil, something that has to be done in order to have the means to do the things they really enjoy. It is inconceivable that work could possibly provide enjoyment in and of itself.

Fear of work usually leads to procrastination, the biggest time, energy, and morale waster there is. Procrastination comes pretty naturally. People use it to escape seemingly overwhelming and unpleasant tasks, to get someone else to do them, or just because they are afraid of failing. As management expert Fred Pryor says, "People procrastinate when they cannot anticipate achievement." Whatever the reason, the result of procrastination is always the same: frustration, anxiety and mediocrity. If you're really intent on failing, at least do it with a little flair. Don't fall victim to such a common, no-class problem as procrastination. Going from a mind-set of "I'll get to it tomorrow" to "I'll do it today" is a tough transition. But it's worth it.

Discipline can be seen, then, as the dual process of "dehorribleizing" work and anticipating achievement. Here are several insights and techniques that should help you once and for all get with the self-discipline program, and tackle (with enthusiasm!) even the most loathsome projects.

The pain/pleasure principle. Like most people, you probably have a little of the child in you: you want it, you want a lot of it, and you want it now. And, like most adults, you've found that in the Real World it rarely happens that way.

Unfortunately, sometimes people have to endure pain before they can enjoy pleasure. Relax, we're not going to get into a puritan guilt or original sin ethic here, and we're not going to suggest you learn how to enjoy pain (unless, of course...oh, never mind).

What we're saying is simply that by understanding that pain often precedes pleasure, and by keeping an eye on the pleasure that will result from a painful activity, you make the activity far less painful. Consider: while working toward an important objective you find yourself under a cloud of anxiety and frustration. Upon successful completion, though, you get money, attention and an internal sense of accomplishment. Let the latter help you through the former. When your task gets particularly trying, stop for a moment and visualize yourself completing it successfully. It's like dangling a carrot in front of a horse.

Sacrifice until it is no longer a sacrifice. This means give up the little things so you'll have time for the big things. For example, if you sacrifice watching television every night (which, considering the pap that appears, shouldn't be so hard) you'll open up a nice chunk of time to spend on your high-priority goals. Once you have filled your previous television time slot with more stimulating activities, you'll wonder how you ever allowed yourself to waste your time so flagrantly.

Look at your own life. You'll be able to see a thousand small sacrifices that could add up to big gains.

Get your second wind. You may understand the second-wind phenomenon from running, or other high-stress athletics. The same dynamic takes effect when you're "working out" in your head. The next time you get so weary you think you can't go on, try to find it within yourself to keep pushing. Don't give in when you feel drained; don't stop when it hurts; don't quit when you feel you can't take it anymore (if you think it will help, hum the theme song from *Rocky*). Soon you'll break the second-wind barrier, and on the other side you'll find a reserve of strength you didn't know you had: an exciting level of focused consciousness and hyperproductivity.

Think of the times in college when you "pulled an all-nighter." Chances are if somebody told you you had to pull one again tonight you'd think, "Impossible, I'll never make it." But when you had to, you did. And if you had to now, you would. That pressure of having to produce makes you push through to your second wind. Unfortunately, most people cannot bring themselves to enter that level of productivity without external pressure. The trick is learning how to put the pressure of having to produce *on yourself.* The result, in addition to getting the work accomplished, is the euphoria and self-satisfaction of knowing that you have entered—and can enter at will—a new plateau of personal power.

Imagine it. Try this exercise before you begin a task. Close your eyes and relax…imagine that you have just finished your project, done an outstanding job, and are basking in the good feeling of having achieved another goal. In your vision, focus on every process you went through to complete the task: the details, the hang-ups, the breakthroughs, the satisfactions, and particularly the elation of finishing and realizing your rewards.

The key benefit of this exercise is that it makes the task seem less intimidating. It will let you see that, yes, you actually are capable of handling it. Where you once felt only dread you may begin to feel a flicker of enthusiasm.

Reward yourself. Or, if you prefer, bribe yourself (this technique is perfect for those of us who don't mind occasionally putting pleasure ahead of principle). The next time you have an unpleasant task to perform, promise yourself a reward for getting it done. The reward could be a dinner out, a day off, or some new clothes...anything that will motivate you. Upon completing your task you will be able to reward yourself freely and without guilt. Whatever you do, don't cheat (maintain *some* pride, for heaven's sake) by giving yourself the reward before you've finished. That would only reinforce your bad habits.

Commit yourself publicly. Get other people involved in your goal with you. For example, if you want to learn a foreign language, ask three friends to monitor your progress every week. They will keep you motivated by encouraging you to stick with your goal, reminding you of your initial enthusiasm when things get tough, and reproaching you if you begin to ease up.*

Become an automaton. This is a nasty, dehumanizing, mentally debilitating technique that just may work like a charm when all else has failed. Automatons don't worry about losing face in front of others, they have no concept of pain or pleasure, and they don't respond to rewards. All they know is...do it.

As our friend David described his morning running routine: "When the clock rings at 5:30, I don't think about how warm it is in my bed and how cold it is outside. I don't think how good I'm going to feel

---

*Getting other people involved in your goals can be particularly powerful if the people you recruit happen to enjoy your failures.

when I'm done. I don't think about maintaining my health or living longer. I allow no issues to even be raised for discussion. I simply reach out and turn off the alarm, sit up and put one foot in front of the other."

Do it for ten minutes. This is the most helpful anti-procrastination trick of all. Obviously, effort is required to start a new project. Likewise, effort is required to shift gears from one project to another. And the effort required to get from the starting block to full speed is greater than that required to maintain full speed. When you sit down to write a report, for instance, you may find that you don't even know where to begin. After a while, however, things start to click and the writing comes more easily.

That's why you can often get going on a procrastinated project by committing yourself to working on it for ten minutes. After ten good, solid whole-hearted minutes (come on, you can take anything for ten minutes), reconsider. If you want to quit, quit. But chances are good you'll realize the job isn't so terrible after all, and you've built up enough momentum to continue.

Break it up. The concept of divide and conquer worked for Alexander the Great and it will work for you. Anything is less intimidating when it is broken into pieces.

If you have a big, intimidating project hanging over your head, don't think in terms of, "I've got to get that project done." That could be sufficiently oppressive to keep you from getting near it until the fearful Night Before It's Due. Instead think, "This morning I'm going to do the statistical analysis on

Table A." That's a more manageable task, and when you're done you'll feel so much better about the project in general that seeing it through, in this step-by-step manner, will be easier than you ever thought possible.

Concentrate. Concentration is the road to your highest levels of analytical and intuitive powers. It not only saves you time by enabling you to process information more quickly, it also increases the quality of your ideas and the sophistication of your mental processes.

There are lots of ways to develop concentration: biofeedback, yoga, meditation, and plain old physical exercise are all good "centering" techniques. The best way to improve your powers of concentration on your work, however, is to tie your concentration development program directly to your day-to-day work requirements. Try the following two-step technique. First, create an environment where you can count on specified periods of quiet. At work, this means directing the receptionist to hold your calls and interruptions for a period of time; at home, it means unplugging your phone or turning on your answering machine.

After creating the proper environment, the next step is to actively center your mind on your work. When it wanders, grab it and drag it back to the topic at hand. Don't give an inch. You may find this focused thinking brutally difficult at first, but soon your mind will get used to it. Try this concentration technique for ten minutes (remember, you can do anything for ten minutes), then extend it to fifteen and twenty minutes. Continue to extend this forced concentration span until you achieve a comfortable and productive level.

How to Decide

The key principle of decision making is simple: *don't put it off.* Efficiency expert Charles Flory estimates that of all the problems that land on a business executive's desk, 15% need to mature, 5% need not be dealt with at all, and 80% should be decided immediately and on the spot. There are several benefits to making a quick decision:

1. You get it out of the way. You save time and energy not worrying about it, not having unnecessary meetings on it, and not gathering unnecessary facts.

2. If you make the wrong decision you have more time to correct it.

3. Some problems are such that any course of action is better than no course of action.

The natural inclination, however, is to avoid making decisions. Why? Because every decision is, by definition, a risk, an attempt to balance potential gains and potential losses—and nobody takes a risk unless he or she has to. But as a professional you *have* to take risks.

Beyond the obvious time and energy economy of timely decisions, there is another interesting advantage. The very nature of quick, decisive action has a quality about it that works in favor of its success. Think about great leaders of history, or great leaders you have known. Even when they are in doubt about a particular course of action, once they commit themselves to it they exude a decisiveness and confidence that sparks the people around them, and actively influences events in their favor. For this reason, a not-so-wise decision made decisively can be more fruitful than a wise decision made after excessive waffling and deliberation.

One excuse many people use to avoid making decisions is "fact-finding," otherwise known as the Paralysis of Analysis. In decision making, as in almost every other phase of business, the Pareto principle holds true: 20% of the facts are critical to 80% of the outcome. Part of being an effective professional is having the confidence and ability to make a decision without having all the facts...because in business you almost never have all the facts.

So when faced with a decision, ask yourself these two simple questions:
1. "Do I need to make this decision now?" Chances are you do.
2. "Do I need more facts to make a valid decision?" Chances are you don't.

When the Shit Hits the Fan

How you react in a pressure-cooker situation says a lot about your character, leadership potential and skill as a professional. And most crisis situations can best be handled by following this one simple principle: no matter how desperate the situation appears, always take the time to step back and compose yourself. Consider the following five points before you do *anything*. They will prevent you from acting irrationally, and may even lead you directly to the best course of action.

1. Don't panic. If you go berserk every time something goes wrong, you will gain the well-deserved reputation as someone who "can't take the heat." If you remain calm and objective, however, you will be perceived as confident and in control. It's a simple, critical matter of image.

2. Clear your head. Sometimes everything goes haywire and appears to be hopelessly out of control. It's easy to let this kind of situation overwhelm you. That's the time to take a walk, go see a movie, or do anything to clear your mind of all the negative energy that can jam your thinking and leave you helpless. When you feel desperation coming on, get away and clear your head. Chances are you'll come back with a new, more realistic perspective.

3. What's the worst that could happen? When the jig's up, ask yourself that question. You could save yourself a lot of needless stress if you realize, at the outset, that the consequences of a catastrophe may not be all that catastrophic. At any rate, you'll know how serious the problem is and where you stand. You'll avoid going off the deep end needlessly.

Another relevant question is, "In five years, what will it matter?" Consider: Will you be a bum living on skid row in five years if you mishandle this predicament, or will it just be a temporary setback from which you can rebound? The answer will stop you from crucifying yourself (unless, of course, the answer is "yes" to skid row).

4. Find the opportunity. In every problem there is an opportunity for growth and gain. The trick is to find it and seize it. Take the problem apart. Look at it from different perspectives. What potential good could come from it? The point is (to dredge up an old cliche), if you've been dealt a lemon, try to make lemonade.

5. Remember life has setbacks. Unfortunately, it really does. And this could be one of them. If that's the case, then deal with the situation in the most mature manner you know. Admit the failure, accept the responsibility, and bounce back as quickly as you can. Don't let a bad set of circumstances destroy you or torpedo all earlier successes. Everyone is vulnerable to setbacks; nobody expects you not to make mistakes.

Creative Nights

One of the best things you can do to improve the chances of success in your career—and your life in general—is to set aside for yourself what we call *creative nights*. Every week or two (it's good to formalize the system, otherwise it's too easy to "never get to it") dedicate an entire evening to stimulating your personal growth and recharging your batteries. There are no strict guidelines as to what you should do on a creative night. Anything from writing in a journal to staring at the stars will suffice, provided you follow six simple rules.

1. Enforce peace and quiet. Set aside an *entire* evening and block out *all* interruptions. Turn off the television, turn off the stereo, and most of all, turn off the telephone. If it helps you to get in the proper frame of mind (heavy theta waves, for you biofeedback buffs), do some meditation, deep breathing, stretching or some other kind of centering exercise.

2. Enjoy yourself. Creative nights require some discipline, but discipline is not the point of the exercise. Don't do anything just because you think it is "good for you." Do things you genuinely enjoy doing.

And do them only so long as you can continue to enjoy them. When you get bored, or the task turns tedious, quit and move on to another activity. Unless a creative night is totally enjoyable, it is counterproductive.

3. Do something constructive. Okay, so you enjoy lying on the couch eating potato chips. That doesn't count. When deciding whether a particular activity is appropriate to a creative night, subject it to two criteria: 1) does it require your active involvement? and 2) does it have lasting value? For instance, if you decide to read a book, read one that will give you more than just entertainment.

4. Expand your boundaries. For example, if you decide to spend your creative night playing a musical instrument, let this be the night you forget about doing finger exercises and learning new material. Let this be the night you *perform* on your instrument. Fantasize that you are performing in front of twenty thousand screaming fans at Madison Square Garden. Relax and open yourself to new methods of expression.

5. Relate it to your career sometimes. Creative nights are very valuable in your career. In fact, we believe they are essential, provided you follow the rules. You'll be surprised at what happens when you spend a night away from your desk, without the day-to-day hassles, distractions and deadlines, thinking exclusively about the big picture of your career.

Be sure you don't work on any urgent or deadline projects during a creative night. Do some thinking on a project that you haven't even started. In fact, this is how every project should be started—with some free-wheeling, unpressured, "big-thinking" thinking.

6. Share it sometimes. It is not necessary to enjoy a creative night alone. Invite a close friend, as long as he or she understands and agrees to the rules. Work on a project together, read to each other, counsel together on the problems in your lives, or have a structured intellectual discussion. A creative night is a wonderful way to get closer to someone.

A problem with creative nights is that they are easy to postpone. You must make them a priority and guard them as the valuable means of personal and professional growth that they are. After you get in the habit of creative nights you will wonder how you ever did without them.

8: The Basics: Reading, Writing, Speaking, Listening

You probably could do all of them by the time you were six years old. However, like most people, you probably don't do them as well as you should, or could.

Reading, writing, speaking and listening are the basics of information input and output. Nonverbal communication is also a factor—and so is intuition, possibly—but for the most part, when we communicate it is usually as a verbal or written function, or some combination of the two. The importance of these basics to you as a person, and a professional, cannot be overemphasized.

Improving your reading, writing, speaking and listening skills is the single most valuable professional-development program you can embark on. In the following pages we will take a look at each of the basics, and tune you in to some insights and techniques that will help you improve your proficiency in each, and your professional effectiveness.

Reading

It has been estimated that business executives spend, on the average, 30% of their working time reading. It makes sense that this statistic would hold true in other professions as well. That means you will probably devote almost one work-year of the next three to just reading.

Obviously, if you can achieve even a small improvement in your reading proficiency, you can net big rewards. Here are three ways to get started. These techniques are particularly helpful if, currently, you do not read as often or as well as you'd like.

1. Develop a reading center. Like most college veterans, you've probably developed the ability to read at many times during the day in many places: at the breakfast table, on the bus, at your desk, in your favorite chair during the evening, in bed before falling asleep. Reading is a great way to pass the time and put dead hours to work, and it is valuable to be able to read in various environments.

For serious, volume reading, however, you should formalize the system a bit by putting together a *reading center.* A reading center is a place in your home or office which is furnished and set aside for the sole purpose of reading.

There are five essential components of a good reading center: 1) Quiet. You must be able to relax in your reading center and count on a block of uninterrupted time. That way, simply being there will signal your mind to put itself in a less distracted, more concentrative mode. You'll be surprised at how powerful this can be. 2) Comfort. But not so much that you want to fall asleep. A recliner or chair with an ottoman is a good bet. 3) Lots of light. Choose a lamp that is bright, but not one that causes a glare. Be sure to position the light so it doesn't create a shadow on your reading material. We're not nit-picking here—lighting is a big factor in your reading capacity and enjoyment. 4) A dictionary. Stop passing over words you don't understand; each new word is an opportunity to improve your vocabulary and to participate more fully in the richness of language. If you want to go whole-hog, consider getting a big, hardbound dictionary on a pedestal, like the library has, and leave it in an open position. (This is great for your image, particularly when combined with pipe, smoking jacket and an old, faithful dog.) 5) A means of recording information. A pen and paper, dictation machine...whatever is convenient for you to record your reactions to what you are reading.

That's all there is to creating a reading center. The best place for your reading center is probably in your home. Put one in your office too, even if it's just a good light and dictionary at your desk. And always be careful to screen out interruptions when using it.

2. Read actively. Nonrecreational reading should never be passive. To get the most out of your reading, you must get involved with it. Underline passages you feel are important. After each chapter or section, sit back for a few minutes to identify your thoughts and feelings, sum up the author's message, and criticize the work. Then record your insights and keep them; you'll be surprised how often you refer to them. Reading this way takes a little longer, but it is so much more productive, hour for hour, that it is well worth the time.

3. Learn speed reading. A lot of people consider speed reading to be a gimmick. It isn't. Almost anybody who has seriously followed a reputable speed reading program will have at least doubled his or her reading rate, and increased comprehension. Most people average a gain of between three and four times their former speed. So, if you *do* end up spending 30% of your working time reading, a good speed reading program may well save you six months' time within the next three years. There are several reputable speed reading courses and home-study programs available. Investigate them.

To take speed reading a step further, one efficiency expert offers a technique for reading 50,000 words a minute. All you have to do is recognize, within one minute, that a 50,000-word book does not suit your purpose, and decide not to read it. Don't fall into the trap of feeling you have to finish every book you start. And, also, avoid the trap of feeling you have to read every word of a book. Often skimming—particularly in non-recreational reading—can give you all the important information a book or article has to offer, at a fraction of the time. This is speed reading at its best.

Writing

The most important professional benefit of good writing skills is that they enable you to make yourself understood. It's no small feat. The professional world is plagued with all sorts of misread instructions, confused agreements and crossed signals due to poor writing. By presenting your ideas clearly in writing, you minimize this kind of commotion in your professional life.

Another benefit of good writing is that when you present your written ideas in a way people can easily understand, you are regarded as being intelligent, even insightful. Good writing impresses people, opens doors and creates opportunities. That's as it should be. By forcing you to think through and organize what you have to say, good writing does make you "smarter."

Good writing is also a proven leadership skill. If you can get to the level in your writing at which you can communicate personality and feeling, you will be able to touch people on an emotional, as well as intellectual, level. This is a great way to motivate people (more on this in a minute).

Clearly, developing good writing skills is well worth the trouble. And, unfortunately, it *takes* a little trouble. Even though writing is a fundamental skill which we have been practicing nearly all our lives, it can be grueling, frustrating labor.

How to Write Good (Well?)

In written communications, as in spoken, we deal in two commodities: facts and feelings. Business writing deals, for the most part, in facts. The primary purpose of a memo, report, contract, instruction or evaluation is to communicate or record data. But even though feelings play the smaller role in this kind of writing, they are not to be ignored. It is a rare memo or report that can't be made more effective by conveying a little personality or point of view.

The point is, facts and feelings are rarely used to the exclusion of the other in writing. The trick is to know how, when, and to what degree, to combine the two.

Facts-oriented business writing is relatively easy, which makes one wonder why so many people do it so badly. When dealing with facts, all you have to do is ask yourself, "What do I want to say?" Write it down. Then ask yourself, "Now, what do I want to say?" And write *it* down. Continue this process, keeping it relaxed and random, until you have said it all. Then go back and put it in order. Find the big ideas, and support them with the small ideas. Add and delete as you see fit.

Once you have supported and ordered your ideas logically, commit them to paper as clearly and objectively as you can. Pretend you are Mr. Spock or one of the phone company's recordings. Lead your reader by the hand; leave nothing open to misinterpretation or misunderstanding.

> Our 1982 sales volume in Europe was down 19% from 1981. There are three reasons for the decline. First, Europe's domestic industries are catching up with our technology. In England, for instance...

This is simple writing, but good writing. And if it is as far as you advance, you will still be well ahead of most people.

To become a *really* powerful communicator, of course, you will have to add feeling to your writing. This is where you can run into trouble. In spoken communication, feelings are communicated through voice inflection and body language, as well as through word choice. In writing, all we have is the latter. Also, since feelings are, by necessity, subjective and intangible, it is difficult to be sure your reader receives the message you think you are sending. For instance, when describing an ingot of steel in terms of its dimensions, weight, and chemical specifications, you can be pretty sure your reader will be able to create a mental image close to what you intend. But if you try to write about the sensual aspect of touching steel, or of watching steel being made, it is impossible to create a precise mental picture. So *forget* about communicating a precise mental picture. Make it your goal to provide a framework upon which the reader can create his or her own mental picture. The reader's resulting personalized image will be much more powerful.

Treat feelings in your writing much the same way you treat facts: clearly and directly. And sparingly. For example:

> I believe it would be a mistake for us to continue directing our resources toward reestablishing dominance in the European market. It's time we cut our losses. This may be difficult to swallow after all the work we have done, but it is a fact we must face.

Injecting a little feeling and personality into your writing can spice it nicely. But be careful. In writing, as in cooking, where a little spice is nice, a lot is rarely better. Don't let emotion overpower your message.

Ten Quick Writing Improvers

1. Make your first sentence short and simple. The most difficult part of writing is getting started. The same is true of reading. So do yourself *and* your reader a favor by making your first sentence short and simple.

This is an advertising technique, but it works in any kind of writing as long as you don't overdo it. Your first sentence doesn't even have to be a sentence. It could be a fragment, a single word, a quote, even a cliche. "Picture this," "The hunters were closing in for the kill,"* and "Let's be blunt" are good examples of the short, engaging first sentence.

2. Vary the lengths of your sentences. Don't use just short sentences. Or long ones. Especially one after the other. That can be very annoying. See what we mean? Give your writing a good, comfortable rhythm by varying the lengths of your sentences. To get the feel for the rhythm in your writing, try reading it aloud.

3. Use subheads. Subheads serve two valuable functions. They break up long bodies of writing, thus making it less intimidating. Also, they index ideas so the reader can locate sections of special interest. Subheads can be useful even in your business letters and routine communications.

4. Economize. Novice writers often make the mistake

---

*This riveter is the opening sentence of Sidney Sheldon's *Rage of Angels*. Of course for every example supporting the concept of the short opening sentence, there is one which blows it apart. One of the most striking of the latter is the opening sentence of Scott Spencer's novel, *Endless Love:* "When I was seventeen and in full obedience to my heart's most urgent commands, I stepped far from the pathway of normal life and in a moment's time ruined everything I loved—I loved so deeply, and when the love was interrupted, when the incorporeal body of love shrank back in terror and my own body was locked away, it was hard for others to believe that a life so new could suffer so irrevocably."

It's hard *not* to continue reading after that.

of overexplaining. Watch your wordiness. Don't worry about saying everything there is to say about your subject.

5. Take a license. The purpose of writing is to communicate. As long as your writing is clear and effective, don't worry about the strict rules of grammar. It is more important that you write in a natural voice.

6. Learn the rules. Of course before you license yourself to break the rules, it's a good idea to learn them—at least the basic ones. Regarding this process, we advise any writer to read three books: *The Elements of Style* by William Strunk, Jr. and E.B. White; *On Writing Well* by William Zinsser; and *Writing with Precision,* by Jefferson Bates. They're the classics.

7. Use a thesaurus. When only the right word will do, a thesaurus is invaluable. Keep it nearby and consult it often. It will not only improve the quality of your writing, but also build your vocabulary. By the way, *thesaurus* means "treasure house"...it's a nice thought.

8. Close with a BANG! Don't just stop writing. Summarize your points, ask for action, state a moral. The best way to make sure your readers are clear about your message is to leave it ringing in their ears.

9. Sleep on it. As Mario Puzo says, "It's all in the rewrite." Don't burden yourself with having to write the perfect first draft. Take advantage of the power of the second or third draft. You'll be amazed at the perspective a night's sleep can give your writing. Your points will come together more coherently, your transitions will tighten, and you'll have no trouble coming up with the "perfect word" that eluded you in earlier drafts.

10. Get a second opinion. And a third or fourth, for that matter. F. Scott Fitzgerald and Ernest Hemingway both gave a lot of credit for their writing to their editor, Maxwell Perkins. Find yourself an editor, someone you respect who will take the time to critique your writing and suggest ways to improve it.

These ten tips will help you improve your writing the first time you try them. But the only way to become a truly powerful writer is to write. Like all skills, writing gets better with practice. Make strengthening your writing ability a priority in your professional development. You'll appreciate the payoffs.

Talking

We all know people are "born talkers." They're the ones who always have the right thing to say in any situation. They can get a whole room's attention at will, and make almost anything sound interesting, if not important.

The "silver tongue" is definitely a professional asset. It's a simple fact of life: people always assume that someone who can talk well necessarily has something to say. On the other hand, you could be the smartest professional on the block, but if you can't put it across, you will sound like a dim bulb.

In the professional environment there are many opportunities to make yourself heard by talking. And there are lots of ways to improve your ability. Here are a few.

1. Be yourself. In Chapter Nine we'll talk about personal honesty as a general basis of professional style, but it's worth jumping the gun to mention honesty in terms of your style of speaking. Some people, particularly young people, go overboard affecting an air of seriousness when speaking in a business situation. Their voices actually get deeper, they enunciate ev-er-y word to perfection, and generally make everyone, including themselves, very uncomfortable. Don't create a new persona when you talk! Except for the demands of subject matter, your style of speaking in a professional setting shouldn't be much different from your style of speaking in a personal setting.

2. Speak professional-ese. Some words and expressions are more appropriate than others in a professional environment. You can use expressions like "window of opportunity" and "hit the ground running" all day long and no one will give it a second thought. But try using a word like *cute* or *darling* and you will be immediately pegged as a lightweight. Women, be particularly conscious of this; more so than men, you have been socialized to speak in feelings-oriented terms. A good rule of thumb for anyone talking at a business level is to be as precise and objective as possible, without sounding like an accountant (that goes for you accountants, too.)

3. Lower the volume. This is a trick, and it works perfectly in meetings or conversations where the excitement level is high. In this kind of situation, the normal attention-getting ploys, such as talking louder or gesturing for attention, won't work. The solution is to pull a reversal: talk softly. Unless you are dealing with pandemonium, it will get attention in a hurry. It's a simple matter of contrast. An added benefit is that you come across as the voice of reason.

4. Involve the listener(s). Don't make it a monologue. If you're getting through to people, you can bet they will want to respond. By soliciting feedback from your listener, you give him or her an opportunity to validate what you have said. For instance, after completing a thought, you might ask, "Has that ever happened to you?," "How do you see it?" or just "Do you understand?"

5. Make eye contact. This is the oldest speaking advice there is; and for good reason—it works. How annoying and alienating it is to have to listen to someone who is looking at the floor or off into space. Some people find looking into another person's eyes to be distracting, even intimidating. If that's you, try looking at the person's forehead or mouth. They'll never know the difference.

6. Show some enthusiasm. If you aren't excited about what you're saying, how can you expect anyone else to be? Enthusiasm is infectious, a phenomenon persuasive people have known about for centuries. If you find it difficult to show enthusiam over what you have to say, maybe you ought to consider not saying it.

7. Sum up. This is absolutely critical. If more people would take time to conclude their business conversations with a summation of what was said, there would be a lot less confusion flying around. It's one of the mysteries of life how two people can come away from a discussion with a totally different idea as to what was said. But it happens all the time. Summing up is an effective safeguard.

A summation doesn't have to be formal, or even conspicuous. A simple "Okay, so what we've agreed on here is..." will suffice.

Formal Speaking

Speaking formally in front of a group—whether delivering a report to a small group or addressing an audience of thousands—is an extension of the same rules and techniques that operate in face-to-face communication. There's an extension of effect, too: when you blow it in a public speaking situation, you've blown it in front of that many more people. Fortunately the same thing goes, on the positive side, when you "blow them away."

There's nothing like "being the presenter" for gaining visibility and respect in your profession. If you're someone who "just hates to get up and talk in front of other people," get over it, you're excluding yourself from too many opportunities.

An excellent system of public speaking is presented in the book *Standing Ovation or Polite Applause?* by Bern Wheeler and Don Davis (see our reading list). While the focus is on large-scale speechmaking, many of the points the authors make are transferable to small-group presentations.

Your Big Roles

From time to time as a professional you are going to run into situations where you absolutely have to come across as a cool customer: when you ask for a raise, go into a job interview, or make an important presentation, for instance.

Never leave these situations to chance. Never just assume you will say the right things. Even when you know, without a doubt, what you want to say, knowing it and saying it remain two different matters ...especially when the heat is on.

So say it beforehand. The best way to prepare for the really special performances of your professional life is to practice your lines until you know them by heart. Start by writing them down. Mentally put yourself in the situation you are about to face. If you are going to ask for a raise, for instance, imagine yourself sitting across from your boss. What are some of the ways you could begin your request? What are his or her possible responses? What are your possible responses to his or her possible responses? Be specific. There are hundreds of variables, of course, but as you "imagine" the situation you will begin to get a feeling for the major issues, and the best ways to address them.

The next step is to actually write a script for your major speeches. In asking for a raise these speeches might be: 1) The opening monologue (breaking the ice and stating the request). 2) How much you want and the three or four major reasons you deserve it (your added responsibilities, seniority, the new business you have generated for the company, etc.). 3) Your rebuttals to his or her likely objections ("There's no money in the budget"). And, very important, 4) what you will say if ultimately you do not get what you want (Will you settle for another salary review in six months? Will you resign?). You might also create a couple of "optional monologues" to use if the situation warrants (for instance, the things you like about your job, or where you see yourself going in the company).

It is important to practice these big speeches *out loud.* Don't just write them down and read them; that just gives you the illusion of knowing them. Actually recite them, even if it's just to the wall.

Obviously, it's impossible to plan for *every* contingency, so don't even try. Besides, it's better to stay a little flexible. If you have a strict scenario in mind when you enter a big role, you will become hopelessly lost the first time events violate your assumptions. The goal of rehearsing is to be able to go into a performance certain you have a clear, defensible position on the major issues, and that you can deliver it clearly and confidently.

Listening

> *The most successful people are the best listeners, not the best talkers.*
>
> —A saying we heard once,
> but we can't remember where

Listening is the most passive of the basics. But it's not as passive as it seems. There is a lot you can do to improve your listening skills.

One of the biggest problems with listening is that most of us have spent most of our lives learning how *not* to listen. It's a matter of survival; there is so much racket in the world we have to be selective as to what we give our attention to. And since "tuned-out" has become such a natural and comfortable state, we sometimes forget to tune back in again, even when we need to.

Another problem with listening is that people talk at a rate of 125 words per minute, while the mind processes information at the rate of 300 words per minute. As a result, your natural inclination as a listener is to race around the speaker, jump to tangential ideas, prepare a response, or mentally criticize what he or she is saying. Unfortunately, while you are preoccupied with your own ruminations, the speaker may have raced ahead of you. And while it is easy to think ahead of a speaker, it's tough to catch up.

With some people, of course, letting your mind wander from what they are saying is a *more* productive use of time (just be careful you don't let your eyes glaze over). It's up to you; in each situation you have to calculate the value of listening versus the consequences of not listening. Most of the time, however—particularly on the job—you'll want, or have, to listen to what is being said to you. Here are six ways to do it better.

1. Consciously concentrate. Work at it. When you enter a situation where you know you have to concentrate, remind yourself of that fact. Bear down, subliminate other thoughts, and put yourself—forcibly if necessary—into a "tuned-in" mode. The simplicity of this technique is deceptive. It works.

2. Look at the speaker. If your eyes drift too long or too often onto other objects of interest, your mind won't be far behind. Also, when you look at your speaker, you should show interest in what he or she has to say. Chances are he or she will be more open and enthusiastic.

3. Don't talk when you're listening. It's something like talking with your mouth full: rude. We all remember the young intellectual in class who felt he or she had to elaborate on everything the professor said. And even though we knew it was a sign of insecurity (on account of what we learned in Psychology 101), it was still a pain in the ass. The point is, even though it's sometimes a good idea to ask questions or add insights to what someone is saying, don't make a pest of yourself.

4. Don't filter out the negative. The good news is that when we listen to what we want to hear, we're all ears. The bad news is that when we hear something that goes against our wishes or assumptions, we tune out. For instance, suppose a colleague tells you, "I'll have that project done by Wednesday if all the materials come in." Because you want the project to be done by Wednesday, you latch on to just the first part of your colleague's statement and make your plans accordingly. It won't be until Wednesday, with the project not done because the materials didn't come in, that you'll remember everything that was said. By then it may be too late.

5. Sum up. This is particularly valuable in those situations where you absolutely *have* to understand what is said. When the speaker comes to a natural pause after concluding his point, paraphrase what he or she said. This will not only help to crystallize the ideas in your mind, but it will give your speaker the opportunity to clear up anything that was miscommunicated. When it's not possible to sum up aloud—such as in a conference or classroom situation—do it in your head.

6. Listen aggressively. Sometimes you have to take charge of a conversation even when you're not the one doing the talking.

Listening aggressively means you force yourself to hang in there every word of the way. Make it your own private game: don't let the speaker get away with you not understanding every detail of what he or she is saying. When a point is not clear, speak up and ask for clarification.

This is a great technique to use on people who ramble. When they realize you are serious about gaining information and not indulging their sloppy communication, they are forced to be more clear. It's also a great technique to use on shy or inarticulate people. Knowing that you—as a listener—have taken charge of the conversation often makes it easier for them to talk.

9: Your Professional Style

As a professional you have two sets of loyalties: one to yourself and one to your organization. Although they are not mutually exclusive, they sometimes conflict, and almost never harmonize. The key to success and satisfaction as a professional in the modern organization is to develop an operating style that reconciles the two as often as possible.

Independence and self-sufficiency are concepts Americans regard highly. Many of our heroes—Henry David Thoreau, Howard Roark, even Johnny Appleseed—are stereotypes of the Great American Loner. The organization, however, is typically seen as the enemy of the individual. We know too well the stifling, dehumanizing effects of the organization on such cultural stereotypes as Willie Loman, Darin Stevens and George Jetson. As a result, most professionals have an underlying hostility for organizational life, and may even entertain the occasional daydream of telling everyone to go to hell.

But for better or worse, the professional world is a world of cooperation. As a professional you *have* to work with other people. It boils down to a simple principle: *the better the people you work with, and the better you are able to work with them, the more you will accomplish.*

But the forces for cooperation are not, as some critics suggest, necessarily forces for conformity. Take heart—the media's stereotypes of professional organizations are largely false. If regimentation ever was a characteristic (and perhaps it was), it is no longer. The trend in today's organization is toward flexibility and accommodation of the individual. So if you are heading out into the Real World expecting to fit into some slot, you're in for a surprise (a pleasant one, we trust): professional life can be pretty much what you want it to be.

Within limits, of course. You are likewise in for a surprise if you expect professional life to be a freeform, I-can-only-work-when-I'm-inspired proposition. The Real World may not be regimented, but it *is* disciplined. Business is still business, and that means every action must be calculated to achieve a goal, and every result must be held up to objective evaluation. Although individual interests are accepted—and even encouraged—they are always superseded by the interests of the organization. And the interests of the organization are not defined democratically.

So where does that leave us? How does one reconcile the conflicting loyalties between self and organization? What is the best way to operate in today's professional world?

The answer is simple and encouraging: there is no "best way." Look at the people you know who have made it as professionals. They run the range of humanity: the humorless "all-business" person, the outspoken roughneck, the diplomat, the charismatic, the barracuda, the backslapping gladhander, the young turk.

Today the central rule of professional style is *play your own game*. Don't try to be someone you're not. If you're not much for small talk, just get right down to business. If you can't tell a joke, don't try (*please* don't try). If you're uncomfortable with the formality of a situation, then be the one to break the ice and lighten things up a bit. The evolving climate of flexibility and diversity in the professional world has opened more room for individuality than ever before.

This is not to say there won't be pressure for you to conform. You're always going to run into the colleague who tries to engage you in football talk (while you may still be trying to figure out how they can dribble such an odd ball), or the boss who thinks if you have a sense of humor you must not be a serious professional. It's natural for people to try to make you into the person they expect you to be. But strangely enough, when you violate their assumptions and resist their pressure they usually end up liking and respecting you more—once they get over the initial shock. They are impressed with your integrity and sense of self. After all, everybody catches on sooner or later to the people who always act the way they think they are expected to act.

The goal, then, is to develop a professional style that is effective in the organization, yet comfortable to you. Luckily you don't have to start from scratch. A lot of people have walked this tightrope before you, and you can learn a lot from their mistakes and failures. In this chapter we will talk about the elements of professional style that we feel are important to those of you who are just starting out. We know—firsthand—that they work.

Assertiveness

You've probably heard the term *assertiveness.* Maybe you think you've heard it too much. Several years ago assertiveness became the trendy concept in self-help circles, and some of the more ardent of the Me Generation have used it as a license for selfishness and insensitivity ever since. In that way assertiveness has been misunderstood. Actually, its basic concept— clarity, honesty and directness in communication —is sound, particularly in the professional world.

Assertiveness is the keystone to an effective professional style. One of the leading proponents of assertiveness in the professional setting is communications expert Larry Schwimmer. Here are three of Schwimmer's most powerful principles of assertiveness. You'll be surprised at how well they work.

1. Use "I" language. This is a good rule of thumb in any communication, personal or professional. "I" language is the technique of acknowledging that what you are saying is a product of your own perceptions. For example, instead of saying to someone, "you were wrong," using "I" language you would say, "I really believe you were wrong."

There *is* a difference. In the first case you are acting as the judge and jury presenting a final verdict, which tends to make the other person resentful and defensive. In the second case you are simply stating your own conclusions, the implication being that there may be circumstances you don't know about that could influence your judgment, and that your judgment is based on your values, which the other person may not share. The "I" language approach is also more honest: there is rarely a situation where you are aware of every potentially mitigating circumstance, and your judgments *are* based on your values, which are relative. The message in both cases is essentially the same, but the style and emotional content are significantly different. Obviously, the tone of any human exchange is often as important as the content; "I" language works like magic to make your communications more cooperative and productive.

To use another example, let's say the man sitting at the desk next to you is clicking his ballpoint pen, and it is really annoying you. Avoid saying something like, "You're really annoying me with that pen clicking." Instead say something like, "I am really annoyed by your pen clicking. Would you please stop?" In the first instance you're bound to put the other person on the defensive. You're practically accusing him of having a premeditated plan to annoy you. Actually, he may have been unaware of what he was doing. In the second response, you are not attacking him personally. Rather, you're saying it's the pen clicking that is annoying you—not him.

"I" language works in many situations: "I'm really upset about what you did," instead of, "You upset me." "I feel you are reneging on the agreement," instead of, "You're deliberately reneging on the agreement." "I feel you're taking advantage of me," instead of, "You're taking advantage of me."

"I" language doesn't guarantee that no one will ever get defensive to what you say or that you'll always get what you want. But it does maximize your chance to get the other person's cooperation. And as a professional your ability to gain other people's cooperation is one of your most important assets.

2. Set limits and consequences. Another valuable principle of assertive communication is to make it clear to other people what your limits are, and the consequences of violating them. Getting back to the guy who clicks his pen: suppose, after repeated requests, he refuses to stop his offensive behavior. It's time to set your limits and issue a consequence. Tell him, "I have already told you that your pen clicking is really bothering me and asked you to stop. I'd like to resolve this between us, but if that's not possible I'm going to the boss and see if he can help us work it out."

With that statement you have made it clear what your limits are ("stop now") and the consequence of violating your limits ("I will go to the boss"). At that point, it's up to him to either stop clicking his pen or risk being exposed to the boss as the clod he obviously is.

Don't get hung up on the simplicity of this example. The key is to let others know what your limits are and the consequences of violating them. Also, there is nothing worse than an "empty consequence," so make sure you are willing to follow through. As the song says, "Don't make promises you can't keep." If you don't honor your limits and consequences, how can you expect anyone else to honor them?

3. Do not take responsibility for other people's reactions to your assertiveness. It's natural, when you're communicating your feelings directly, to worry about how the other person is going to take it. Is he or she going to get angry and stop liking you? Will you hurt his or her feelings?

There is always the chance that you will alienate someone, and from time to time it will happen. But if being liked by everyone is what is most important to you, you'll soon find that you won't be doing your job effectively. Assertive people want to be respected first and liked second. It's natural, especially if you become a manager, to find that not everyone will respond to your requests as if you were best friends. But as a professional your role at work is not to be best friends.

When you are assertive and honest in an open way, people will respect you for your directness. They'll know you don't speak out of both sides of your mouth. They'll trust you. And most of the time they'll respond favorably to your assertive style of communication. Take the pen-clicker. He might very well say, "Boy, I was just teasing. If it really bothers you, of course I'll stop." In that way assertive communication fosters mutual respect and maximizes the cooperation you'll get from others. Best of all, it helps you to be seen as the professional you are.

Playing It Straight

When Jeff was visiting a friend back in his home town a couple of Christmases ago, the friend's father and mother stopped by. The father, a guy who had worked most of his life in a small business, and whose recent retirement symbolized his abandonment of the hope that he would ever be more than a disappointment to himself, started telling Jeff and his friend that in order to make it in this world you have to be a shyster "just like the rest of them." He said you have to take what you can get, just like everybody else.

Perhaps you share that view. Between the ravings of embittered cynics like Jeff's friend's father, and the twisted stereotypes of television and pop culture, it's easy to get the idea that it is accepted behavior for businesspeople to lie, cheat, sell out their friends and (if you watch a *lot* of television) hire goons to murder the competition.

But this is *not* accepted behavior, nor is it common. The truth is that in the Real World most people are honest. Besides the occasional white lie, over-exaggeration or lame excuse, most people really *do* play it straight most of the time. So don't buy into the "me against them—winning is everything" hype; it simply doesn't work. It would be nice to be able to say the reason it doesn't work is that dishonesty inevitably backfires or that crime does not pay in the new professional world. But often it does pay, in the sense that people "get away" with it. There has to be a better reason to be honest, and there are a few of them in fact: 1) You don't have to cheat to win. You *can* make it by playing it straight. Again, lots of people have and lots of people do. 2) Most people feel an honest outrage against cheaters. And in the Real World, once you show yourself to be dishonest, you lose forever the capacity to be trusted. Also—and this can get really ugly—you are fair game for your fellow cheaters who will jump on you even harder in an attempt to disassociate themselves, and purge their own souls. 3) Part of the fun is knowing you played it straight. It's the classy way to go. You have respect for yourself, and you're freed from the burden of always having to look over your shoulder.*

The best way to maintain your honesty in business is to surround yourself with people who do the same. If you work with dishonest people it's too easy to justify their behavior with an excuse like "well, that's the way it's done," and pick up some very bad habits. Once you pick up these habits they are very hard to break.

Gossip

Dishonesty in business is not always as flagrant as a broken contract. There is a far more subtle and pervasive form: office gossip. It goes without saying that if you conduct yourself with integrity, you won't go around talking about other people behind their backs. But this couldn't in good faith be called a book on the Real World if we didn't acknowledge that even the best of us enjoy indulging in a little muckraking sometimes. As essayist Lance Morrow says: "From the morning of the first individual folly of the race, gossip has been the nattering background noise of civilization: Molly Goldberg at her kitchen window, Voltaire at the water cooler. To say that gossip has been much condemned is like saying that sex has sometimes been held in low esteem. It is true, but it misses some of the fun of the thing."

So if you do indulge in a bit of gossip now and then, relax; you're carrying on a fine old tradition. To minimize the risk, however, there are a couple things to keep in mind. First of all, don't say anything about

---

*Also, you won't have to worry about going to Hell when you die.

anybody that you would mind terribly him or her finding out about. This is a convenient distinction between simple recreational gossip and the more malicious variety. Also, limit your gossip partners to people you can trust. A good gossip partnership can actually be healthy. It gives you and your partner the opportunity to get together and think through your feelings about someone's behavior, and thereby learn from it.

Another good reason to limit your gossiping has nothing to do with morality. It's a simple matter of style. By keeping your distance from the office gossip mill, you become immune to your position in it. Some people expend more time and energy on office politics than they do on their job. They are obsessed with the daily Who's In/Who's Out, and forever anxious about their own standing. It's a sign of a loser. In order to make an impact in the Real World, you've got to risk being on The Out from time to time. People can sense when you are indifferent to the "what are they going to think?" trap. They respect it; it's a sign of a leader. And as long as you do what you do with integrity and respect for others—and show that you can be trusted to keep confidential information confidential (no matter how much fun you could have with it)—you will be above reproach.

Accountability

One of the most valuable lessons you must learn as a professional is that you are accountable for fulfilling your responsibilities, no matter what the mitigating circumstances. In college you may have been able to get away with excuses like "I didn't know we were going to be tested on Chapter Eight through

Ten" or "my girlfriend left me and I'm a mess" or "my
dog ate my term paper." (This last excuse was actually used by a student in one of Jeff's political science
classes...and accepted by the professor.) But in the
Real World, forgetting, misunderstanding, assuming,
and being let down by other people (or animals) do
not get you off the hook.

Being accountable for your own work is tough
enough, but it gets really stressful when you have to
start being accountable for the work of your subordinates. People—even the most trustworthy and competent people—sometimes make stupid mistakes, and
it's impossible to predict them. Say, for example, you
are at a client's office delivering a presentation and
you realize that your secretary has neglected to
include the all-important budget figures. You told your
secretary twice to be sure to include them, and clearly
conveyed the importance of everything being right for
this presentation. But now you are standing in front
of your client and it is perfectly clear that for one
reason or another the budget figures are not to
be found.

There are a couple of ways to handle this situation. The way *not* to handle it, however, is to blame
it on your secretary, as if its not being your direct
mistake absolves you. Your client doesn't care if your
secretary is incompetent or had a bad day. The internal workings of your organization are your problem,
and it's your responsibility to see that your organization does its job properly. All your clients care about
is that you were supposed to bring the budget
figures...and that you did not bring them. Far better
is to say something like, "Obviously we had a breakdown in preparing this presentation. I'll bring you the

budget figures by the end of the day. I'm sorry."

Another common excuse "unprofessionals" use to escape their accountability is "there was nothing I could do about it." Suppose, for example, you were responsible for getting an important package to an air courier service for delivery the next day. The deadline for getting the package to the courier is six o'clock. You arrive at five-thirty only to find that the courier has changed its deadline to five o'clock. The plane your package had to be on left a half-hour ago. There's nothing you can do. You turn around and walk out.

You know everyone at your office is going to be terribly upset, so by the time you arrive there the next morning, with the unshipped package in your hands, you've rehearsed your story a thousand times in your head. *"I am so upset,"* you announce, eager to align yourself with everyone else, "Air Courier up and changed their deadline schedule to five o'clock and didn't tell any of their customers about it. The deadline has always been six o'clock and suddenly I go in there last night and they tell me they moved it up to five. How was I supposed to know?"

That may *sound* like a good enough excuse, but it falls far short on many counts. First of all, as the person in charge of seeing that packages are delivered, you should have chosen a more dependable air courier, or developed a relationship with them whereby they would have given you notice of a scheduling change.

Second, you assumed that since your deadline had always been six o'clock, it would always be six o'clock. That's assuming too much. Considering the importance of this package you should have called the courier to double-check, leaving nothing to chance.

Third, you accepted defeat far too easily. This was

your biggest mistake. When Air Courier turned out to be an impossibility, you didn't check with other air courier companies. Worse yet, you didn't call your boss, thus precluding any opportunity he or she may have had to do something about it (like hand-deliver it via a commercial flight if it's important enough, or at least call the recipient and minimize the damage). Instead, because you felt you were covered ("How was I to know?"), you either didn't think to do anything else, or didn't want to bother. But a big part of being a professional is knowing when and how to ad lib—and you are responsible to do it. Things rarely go exactly the way they are supposed to go. If you throw your hands up in defeat at the first roadblock you run into—even if it's due to someone else's mistake or unforeseen circumstances—you will never earn the "can-do" reputation you need to be a respected and trusted member of your organization.

Keep accountability foremost in your mind as you enter the Real World. When things go wrong, don't react, as so many do, by looking for excuses or crutches to cover your butt. Your first reaction should be to do what you can to put things back on course, or mitigate the damage. After that, look at the situation with an eye toward seeing what you could have done to avoid it altogether, and thereby ensure that you'll never do it again.

And finally, prepare to take your medicine.

Taking Your Medicine

As we've said before, nobody expects you not to make mistakes. In today's organization a person who is willing to risk making a mistake is more valuable than someone who is afraid to take any action. Successful people usually make more mistakes than people who fail...but they also have more successes. They operate on the proven principle that one success can outweigh ten failures.

Unfortunately, knowing this still does not make failure easy to deal with. It's awful having to face people who were hurt or let down by your mistake. But there is a professional way to handle it.

First, never try to cover it up. You made a mistake, it is probably obvious to everyone, and you are accountable for it. So admit it. It's a drag having to deal with someone who refuses to acknowledge a mistake or becomes defensive over it.

Second, show some remorse. It's almost as bad as refusing to admit your mistake to refuse to admit that it has done damage. Never trivialize a mistake or slough it off with an "oh well, everything will work out." If people think you don't care about the mistakes you make they will have no faith in your motivation to improve. There has to be an emotional catharsis. Your mistake *has* upset things; you must show that it has upset you too. You don't necessarily have to throw yourself on the floor and wail, but it might not be a bad idea to approach your boss and say something like, "I know I really messed things up, and I want you to know I'm sorry." He or she will respect you for it.

Lastly, give assurance it won't happen again. That's the bottom line. If you've learned enough from a mistake that you won't make it again, then it was worth it. Make sure the people around you know you have turned your mistake into a good lesson.

But what if your mistake wasn't exactly an honest

one, but the result of rank negligence or insubordination? Even in an embarrassing and incriminating case like this, honesty and accountability are the best policies. For instance: "I know I was supposed to get the bids in writing, but I was under the gun and thought I could let it slide this time. It's caused a lot of problems, I know. I'm really sorry. It won't happen again."

Handling your failures in this manner can actually enhance your position in your organization. You're demonstrating accountability.

Getting Fired

It *can* happen. And if it does, you'll probably be shocked, depressed and furious—maybe even vengeful. You'll be embarrassed to tell your family and friends. Your confidence will plummet; in fact, you may feel like a total loser.

But take heart. The negative attitude toward firing is slowly beginning to change in the professional world. With job-changing such an accepted practice, employers are forcing "the job change" with less compunction. Likewise, they are more willing to hire people who have been fired from another job. Since it's happening more often, it pays to be prepared.

Unfortunately, Jimmy wasn't. Here's how he handled his termination: "Almost as hard as facing up to my termination was facing my friends and family. There's no easy way to explain away being fired, especially when you had just been riding on top of the world. So I didn't even try. Instead, I took another approach: I lied through my teeth. I told everyone I had quit, had a falling out with the president, discovered 'something' in the company that told me I should leave, or had a better offer elsewhere which fell through. NO WAY would I let on that I had been canned. I just couldn't admit what would appear to others as obvious failure."

If you're ever fired, you may be tempted to handle it the same way, especially if you feel you haven't been treated fairly. And firing is not always fair. Your employer's reasoning may be arbitrary and capricious. Or perhaps you were not warned or given an opportunity to improve. For the most part, however, if you're let go, it's for good reason: your performance has slipped, you've stopped delivering results, you're causing turmoil with clients or suppliers, you've become too difficult to work with, or you simply no longer fit in. Whatever the reason, termination is a sure sign that barriers have become insurmountable. A change is in order.

The change is usually healthy for both parties. When you're let go your future frees up. A space is created for you to reassess your goals, get to know yourself better, and explore new career opportunities. Once you get through the initial difficulty, you may come out of it rejuvenated and back on the right track, with your life more in control. As Jimmy recalls, "If I hadn't gotten sacked I'd probably still be working as a junior executive making $18,000 a year...and thinking I was doing *real* good. When I lost my security blanket, I got a golden opportunity to find out what I was made of, and how far I could go. Ironically, getting fired is now one of the best stories I have to tell. In fact, I recommend that everyone get fired at least once. It just may do for you what it did for me!"

Initiative

David, an acquaintance of Jeff's, was hired as a shortorder cook at a restaurant in Rapid City, Michigan. A dead-end job, right? Not for David. David's a bright guy, and after serving up a few thousand sandwiches, knishes and eggcreams, he began seeing some weak spots in the system. Rather than ignoring the deficiencies ("It's not my job") or complaining self-righteously to his co-workers ("Whoever designed this kitchen didn't know what he was doing"), he did the unexpected: he developed several specific, realistic recommendations for changing the food service system, wrote them up—complete with diagrams and reasons why—and took them, in person, to the president of the company that owned the restaurant.

David's actions would be viewed by some as impertinent (after all, who is a rookie sandwich-boy to tell the president of a restaurant chain how to improve his operations?), but the president didn't think so. In fact, he was so impressed he soon made David the kitchen manager. And now, two years later, David is vice president in charge of operations for the restaurant chain—so valued that he has been put on a lucrative stock ownership plan to help ensure his continued loyalty.

To be successful as quickly as possible you must do what David did—take charge of your career. Always look for ways to extend your authority and influence in your job. Consider your job description to be a definition of the base of your responsibilities, not the boundary. Any time you see a way, beyond your current duties, to make yourself more valuable to your organization, do it. If you see a way to make your job easier—and therefore more efficient—suggest the change to your superiors. They know that you know more than they do about how you can be most productive.

This approach of "grabbing opportunity" and "grabbing knowledge" is essential for a new professional. Remember, your boss is not a trained teacher. Unlike a college professor, he or she may not be ready to give you a new assignment, or shepherd you through one every time you're ready. As Jimmy recalls about his first job, "I didn't have the luxury of a boss with enough spare time to show me the ropes. I was in a small company where many hats were worn by few people. In order to learn the fundamentals of the business, increase my value to the organization, and get ahead, I had to learn on my own. I had no choice but to read everything I could get my hands on, dig through old files, ask too many questions, and do whatever else was necessary to get an insight into the nature of the business. I loved my job, so I wanted to learn every detail. Also, my boss was supportive of my all-out effort. Had I waited for everything to be broken down and explained, I might still be doing my first assignment—packing books."

Don't wait to be trained! Training is a process that you must ultimately take charge of yourself.

Your Look

In the past few years there has been a lot of talk on the subject of how to dress as a professional. If you feel you need help in this area, by all means read one of the many books on the subject (see our reading list). Personal appearance is not an incidental; no matter what your profession, you'll have a better chance of success if you dress and present yourself in a manner considered appropriate.

It is not necessary, however, to get compulsive about it. "Dress-for-success" books and consultants usually oversell the importance of clothing to career advancement...often at the expense of intelligence, competence and ambition. Image is oversold in our society in general, and today's professional world is filled with "empty Brooks Brothers suits"* whose talents don't extend much further than dealing effectively with dry cleaners. So don't spend a fortune on clothes, jewelry and expensive haircuts thinking that is the key to success. You may look like a million bucks, but you won't necessarily make a million bucks. To really score big you're going to need some of the other professional attributes, too, the ones that are downright ugly to look at, like brains and guts.

If you are still sporting roadie T-shirts, jeans, sneakers and turquoise jewelry, however, it's time you considered other options. While the slob look can work quite well in college, it won't work in the Real World. Some college students achieve the slob look by design; they study it and take pains to achieve it. If that's your story, you're not in too much trouble. At least you understand that your physical image is a means of communication which can, like speech, be controlled. Just be aware that to become a professional you will have to communicate a different image. You're in real trouble, however, if you're one of the people who has achieved the slob look by default, by simply being too

---

*What Madison Avenue used to call account executives who did little more than carry artwork back and forth from the agency to the client.

lazy to take care of yourself. To you, our advice is to snap out of it—quick. If you're still comfortable looking like a slob, you are in imminent danger of becoming one.

Not taking your appearance seriously can hurt you enormously, especially if you are entering a profession that requires adherence to traditional, conservative styles. The following true story about two aspiring professionals illustrates just how much it can hurt.

Tom and Bill were good friends, and had just graduated from Princeton with degrees in accounting. Both were above-average students and well-liked. Tom was outgoing, athletic and always took time to look good. Bill, though also outgoing, was a bit overweight and paid less attention to his appearance. After graduation, both Tom and Bill interviewed with all the Big Eight accounting firms. Tom received several job offers (and accepted one), while Bill got nothing but rejections. After one of his unsuccessful interviews, Bill's interviewer leveled with him and told him why. The man said, "Bill, we have no doubt that you could do a good job, but in all honesty we can't hire you because we don't feel you would present the right image to our clients."

Bill got the message and immediately went on a self-improvement kick. He got a haircut, lost some weight and bought a couple of new suits. This is when things went from bad to worse. He scheduled a second round of interviews, this time with a number of privately-held accounting firms, but still was not able to land a position. When he received his final letter of rejection, he called the personnel director at a company where he thought he had made a strong impression and asked why he had not been hired. The interviewer answered that the company had considered Bill carefully, but could not figure out why none of the Big Eight firms had hired him. They assumed the other firms had discovered something negative about Bill that they had overlooked, and were reluctant to take any chances.

This is typical of the timid attitude found in a certain ilk of large companies. But in the Real World, sometimes it happens this way.

A bad personal appearance may not hurt you like it hurt Bill, but will most definitely have a negative impact. Make sure you look the part you want to play.

So what *is* the appropriate image for an up-and-coming Young Achiever like yourself? That depends, for one thing, on the field you are entering. For example, lawyers, accountants, and business executives usually wear conventional business suits. This standard is loosening in some circles, but it is still safe and accepted. Doctors and dentists get to wear those groovy white lab coats. Field engineers wear very expensive yet casual outdoor clothes, like the stuff from L.L. Bean. Architects and commercial artists must show a little flair (otherwise no one will think they have any talent). And college professors can still get away with affecting a disdain for appearance by holding out for the slob look.

The part of the country you're working in also has something to do with how you should look. Cowboy boots with a suit may work in Texas, but in New York you'll just look like you're trying to look like you're from Texas. It's surprising how different professional styles of dress are in various parts of the country. Make sure you know what to pack.

And of course the classic rule of thumb on dressing for success still holds true: dress for the job you want, not for the job you've got.

It will help you if, within the context of a look that is appropriate, you show a little flair. Try to develop a style that is original and distinctive, then stick with it. There are numerous elements to work with; for example, a certain color, fabric, or tailoring style such as pleated pants or skirts, or vested suits. When people can begin to identify you by a certain "look," you will have gone a long way in achieving professional visibility.

Professional Visibility

It's not enough to just be good at what you do; you also have to be seen being good at what you do. And that takes effort. Most people—especially those at the top—are too concerned with what they're doing themselves to pay much attention to the underlings. As one company president is quoted as saying about his management trainees, "The ones who are stand-outs will stand out. The ones I don't notice probably aren't worth noticing."

You have to *work* to get people to notice you, there's no way around it. You can't be Casper Milquetoast or Molly Modest and expect to rise to the top. Think of yourself as a product in the marketplace; as with any product, the fastest way to become known is to advertise. Advertising a product requires attention to two criteria. The first is the content, or meat, of your message—what you actually have to "say" about yourself. Remember, ultimately you can't fool anyone; you can only promote what is there. Don't oversell yourself. The second is the frequency with which you deliver your message.

We've already talked about personal appearance as an element of professional visibility. It also fits very nicely into our advertising analogy, because it strongly addresses both advertising criteria: 1) it denotes the quality of the "product" (quality products usually come in quality packages), and 2) since it is always visible wherever you go, it has great frequency.

Here are four more elements of visibility.

1. Take credit for your work. You don't have to circulate a memo announcing your every success, but don't downplay them either. (And never take credit, no matter how slight, for something you didn't do.) False modesty can be more offensive than bragging. It's all a matter of style. Successful people are generally comfortable with praise, so learn how to accept it graciously.

2. Be a promoter. This relates to your ability as a speaker. Usually it's not the person who thinks of an idea, but the one who presents and promotes it, who gets the greatest recognition. This is as it should be. A person who is able to sell an idea that would otherwise lie fallow deserves the greater visibility.

3. Make sure they know your name. If you expect to go places, it's important that the top brass know your name and can associate it with your face. When you start working with a new firm, your very first objective should be to introduce yourself to the ultimate decision makers. Always use the name you like to be called: Rob instead of Robert, for instance. Nicknames are okay in the Real World because they set you apart from the rest of the crowd. They are also more personable and easier to remember.

4. Sign your name clearly. Don't get carried away with a scribbled signature—it's all ego. One big source of error in business is bad penmanship. If you fail to write legibly nobody will think it's because you are too busy or important. They'll just think it's because you're pretentious, and they'll be right.

Taking a Stand

If you have an opinion on a subject, and it is appropriate for you to state it, then state it and stand by it. Obviously, when other people disagree with your point of view, it's tempting to back down and see it their way (particularly if the other point of view happens to belong to your boss). But it never pays to go against your own judgment, even when you are badly outnumbered.

This is not to say you should never change your mind. If someone can present an argument that refutes your position, of course you should change. But unless that happens don't budge, don't teeter-totter between positions, and don't ride the fence. Unwavering confidence is a sure sign of a professional.

But what it if turns out, when all is said and done, that your position was wrong? So what! You had the confidence to stick with your beliefs until the facts showed otherwise. Take it gracefully, acknowledge where your thinking was misdirected, determine what you learned, and carry on. You can get through the embarrassment. In the long run you'll be respected far more for this approach than for one that smacks of "yes-ism." Besides, if it turns out your position was right, you're the hero. Next time they'll listen more closely.

On the other hand, consider the possible outcomes of backing off and falling in line with the prevailing opinion. If you were originally wrong but allowed yourself to be muscled into the right point of view, you still haven't gained much. Everyone knows you bowed out not because you saw the merits of the winning viewpoint, but because you had no faith in your own. You know—as does everyone else—that you deserve no credit for being right.

Which leads us to the worst position of all: you were originally right but abandoned your point of view. Now you're the big loser. You lost a golden opportunity to display your perception and talent. You sold out your position to be with the majority, and it got you nowhere.

Kick-Ass Confidence

When you win, nothing hurts.

—Joe Namath

This technique involves taking a stand one step further. When you're absolutely sure of something— you've done your homework, looked at it from every angle, and really believe you're right—take a chance! Declare to the world you are going to be the winner.

Kick-ass confidence is the power that comes from having successfully psyched yourself up for a big challenge. Beyond that, it is a device, an offensive tactic that you have probably seen used often, particularly by sports figures (remember the Joe Namath story?) and politicians. For example, in the 1980 Democratic party primaries, Jimmy Carter said of his opponent Ted Kennedy, "I'll whip his ass." Even though Carter was at his all-time low in popularity when he said it, and the race could have gone either way, there was no question that old Jimmy really felt it. Teddy undoubtedly felt it, too, in the form of a little shudder down his spine. As it turned out, Jimmy was the overwhelming winner (of that round anyway).

This illustrates part of the magic of kick-ass confidence: it creates an energy flow that actually increases your success potential. It creates converts of the uncommitted—most people are happy to follow someone who seems to know where he or she is going. It also works to intimidate your opponents. Sometimes as a professional you will be in a situation of flat-out competition where there is one winner and one loser. In those situations, as in a competitive sport, it is acceptable behavior to do everything you can, within the rules, to win…and that includes undermining your opponent's confidence.

Another powerful aspect of kick-ass confidence is that when you predict your success, then achieve it, it makes a big impression on everyone. People wonder if maybe you know something they don't—and a mystique is created about you.

Kick-ass confidence is obviously a risky strategy, and if you use it too often you will begin to sound like Muhammad Ali (although any of us would do well to have his record.) That's showbiz. Remember, too, kick-ass confidence can backfire if you lose. But even with all the risks, it is still well worth it in the right situations.

Negotiation and Cooperation

*If I give you my idea and you give me yours,
then we now each have two ideas, and together
we have four.*
—Gerard I. Nierenberg

Gerard I. Nierenberg, author of *Fundamentals of Negotiation* and father of modern negotiation practice, defines negotiation simply as the process of "two people coming together for agreement." As a professional you will be involved in coming to agreement constantly: every time you accept an assignment from your boss, arrange a deadline, solicit help, make a purchase, write a contract, or ask for the day off. To be a professional is to be a negotiator.

The key to negotiating an agreement is that, as Nierenberg says, "In a successful negotiation everybody wins." This is a rather startling idea, particularly for a neophyte professional. In many ways our society is built on the concept that for there to be a winner there has to be a loser. It's true in sports by definition, it's true in politics by custom, it's true in war by default.

But that's not the way it works in business. In business relationships both sides have interests in common, and when those interests are achieved, both sides win. So when you approach a negotiating situation, try to see where your individual interests and the individual interests of your opponent overlap. Your most obvious common interest is in establishing or maintaining a relationship with each other, otherwise you wouldn't be negotiating. For example, when you approach your boss to ask for the day off to go skiing, your interest is in going skiing on a workday. Your boss's interest is in seeing that you are productive. These two sets of interests may seem to be mutually exclusive; after all, you can't work and ski at the same time.* But also look at where your interests overlap.

---

*Notwithstanding a few of the more treacherous slopes of Aspen Highlands.

You, too, want to be as productive as possible, because you want to advance in your job. And your boss wants to be flexible with you, because that's the only way you will remain productive. Viewed in this way, you have a lot in common, and if you can find this common ground together, you'll have no problem working out a solution that is satisfactory to both of you. (Bring your boss skiing, and take your work with you.)

The quickest way to sabotage a negotiation—and with it a relationship—is to push too hard to try to get something for nothing. Get rid of the notion that in order to succeed in a negotiation you have to make a big score. Taking advantage of another person just gives the illusion of scoring. You may have scored, but you have also created a person who is intent on *evening* the score. That means you'll have to bear the long-term burden of keeping your guard up— ultimately you will have paid very dearly for your "advantage." If, for instance, your boss feels your request for a day off is part of an overall strategy on your part to work as little as possible, he or she will be inflexible. Likewise, if you feel your boss wants to squeeze as much work out of you as possible regardless of your feelings, you will be very reluctant to do any more than the bare minimum. In either of these relationships, you both lose.

Uncooperative relationships can endure, but they never work very well. They are too riddled with rules, suspicion, selfishness and inflexibility to be productive. Surprisingly, though, many people feel that this is the way business ought to be done. They feel if a person they are dealing with isn't at least slightly resentful of them, then they must not be getting the best deal.

Most people *do* appreciate the value of a cooperative, trusting relationship. But often, even people who appreciate the value of these relationships don't know quite how to go about negotiating one. It's human nature to approach another person with suspicion; anyone who has lived in the Real World any length of time knows firsthand that people can be very dangerous. So when you're trying to negotiate a cooperative relationship with someone, don't be surprised if you run into initial hesitation. The implicit demand is "You first. You extend yourself to me and I'll extend myself to you."

When you run into this attitude—and you will, a lot—our advice is take them up on it! Go ahead and be the first to extend yourself. The worst that could happen is they will take advantage of you. Or you may find that they are not sufficiently experienced to handle a cooperative relationship. Either way it's probably not the end of the world, because many relationships that start out badly can turn into productive, creative, enjoyable and lasting partnerships. Provided you're not betting the farm the first time out, it's worth the risk. In fact, it's the only way to go.

Everything is Negotiable

Most people set terms for entering into dealings with other people. Stores set prices on their merchandise, companies set vacation and compensation policies, vendors set fees, delivery schedules and payment terms. These policies are usually printed up in very legal terminology in brochures or on the backs of contracts—the obvious implications being "take it or leave it." Many people, particularly novice professionals, accept these terms at face value and never think to attempt to negotiate them.

On a mass marketing scale, such as with grocery and department stores, non-negotiable prices are a necessity (in fact, price standardization is credited with making mass merchandising possible), so we're not suggesting you dicker over the blue light special at K-Mart. But in most cases, particularly in the professional world, terms are set merely as a matter of convenience. In those cases where the buyer/seller contact is more personal, a negotiated agreement is always an option—especially when the alternative is "leave it," where everybody loses.

When negotiating a purchase, for example, a vendor may be perfectly happy to give you a price break if you give him or her a break on the delivery deadline or payment terms. Everything is negotiable in nonfinancial transactions, too. For instance, if you are a person who needs a little more than the customary two weeks of vacation time a year, try approaching your boss with the offer of working five Saturdays in return for an extra week off, or offer to do a special project that will get you out of the office for a few days.

The point is, there are lots of ways to get what you want in the Real World, provided you are willing to give in return.

10: Professional Partners

Among the scores of people you deal with as a professional, a few will stand out. They are the people with whom you will form more than a casual relationship, with whom you will work closely and depend on over an extended time. Your boss is one, your secretary is another, and others include your close colleagues, suppliers, clients and technical advisers. Think of these people as your *professional partners*. With each of them you form a sort of mini-team, complete with shared goals, shared responsibilities and shared rewards.

But despite the positive connotation of the word "partner," professional partnerships are not necessarily positive. Just as you can't pick your relatives, sometimes you can't pick your partners. And lots of people, due to one circumstance or another, find themselves in partnerships with people they neither like nor work well with. Like sour marriages, relationships like this can endure for years.

Your professional partnerships are far too important for you to allow them to be anything but positive and productive. By understanding the nature of these unique relationships, and the role you play in each, you will be in a better position to turn them into the powerful supports they ought to be. Here are three characteristics of every professional partnership.

1. It is subordinate to a goal. A professional partnership is never an end in itself. Nobody goes to work every day just to enjoy the fellowship; conversely, no one does business with friends just to make money. There has to be an objective purpose—to build a business, to do a job, to make money...whatever. And if that purpose is lost, the partnership becomes unproductive and should be terminated.

That's not as cold as it may sound. When a professional relationship ends, it does not necessarily mean that all nonprofessional ties should also be broken. Lots of once-successful professional partnerships have turned into lifetime friendships. But only after the professional aspects—and all their ramifications—have been dissolved.

2. It has emotional aspects. It's true that some people feel emotions are out of place in the professional world. They sublimate their feelings and resent having to deal with the feelings of others. Don't buy it. Any time one person makes contact with another person, emotions are involved. And although emotions will never play the role in your professional life that they do in your personal life, you should open yourself up to emotional contact with a professional partner, whether it be a shared interest or sense of humor, simple warmth, or a full-fledged friendship. Personal contact with your professional partners not only makes life more enjoyable, but it is the only basis upon which true professional cooperation and trust can grow.

3. It is 50-50. No business relationship can endure where one side gains at the expense of the other, at least not for long. Effective professional partnerships are based on mutual gain. That is a simple, inviolate rule of professional partnership, yet it is often overlooked, especially by novices.

As you develop your professional partnerships, particularly the more important, long-term ones, keep in mind that their quality determines, more than any other single factor, the quality of your accomplishments. Good professional partnerships, like personal partnerships, require effort and commitment. Tune in to each of your partnerships. Be sensitive to their status, and take an active role in keeping them productive and fulfilling.

The Boss

In the conventional view the boss is the enemy: someone who gives orders, denies requests, yells, points out your mistakes, and makes you do things you don't want to do (like work, for instance).

Actually a good boss does all these things...and a lot more. Your boss should be a support in your professional life. He or she should be on your side, and recognize that a big part of his or her job is seeing that you grow in yours.

In college you took pains to see that you got the good professors (or was it the easiest? We forget.) Likewise, in the Real World, although admittedly you will have less choice in the matter, you should do what you can to work under a good boss. A good boss performs four key functions:

1. Makes it clear what is expected of you.
2. Lets you know how you are measuring up.
3. Shows you how to improve your work.
4. Prepares you for higher responsibilities in your organization.

As a professional, you have a right to expect this, and if your boss is failing you—whether through indifference, incompetence, or insecurity—you should consider firing him or her. It's no joke. Firing your boss means parting company, with you, of course, being the one to leave. It is a last-resort option, but if you're serious about professional success, you may decide at some point in your career that it's your best option. Perhaps if you are in an otherwise satisfying job, you may be able to develop other supports to serve the functions your boss is not serving. And, conversely, a good boss could be the deciding factor in keeping you at a job that may not have everything else going for it.

Mentors

A *mentor* is your own personal teacher, counselor and guide in your profession. Usually it is somebody who has "been there," who recognizes your potential and is willing to make a commitment to helping you achieve it. Some people never have a mentor; others have two or three in the course of their careers. A good mentor is one of the most important partners you can have in the early stages of your career.

But be careful: mentorship is the one professional partnership that breaks most of the rules, because it is *primarily* emotional. A mentor relationship is something like a parent/child relationship. You will look up to and admire your mentor much as you did your parents when you were a small child. You will want to prove your worth and make him or her proud. Likewise, your mentors will see you as a child, raw material for them to mold and nurture. And, like parents everywhere, they will try to protect you from the mistakes they made, see that you get the things they never had, and even—and this is the toughest part—discipline you.

A mentor relationship is also like a lover relationship: it's tough to find one by looking, yet you'll never find one unless you open yourself up to it. As the opportunities arise, however, there are a few evaluations you can make of prospective mentors. Most important is to determine whether he or she is someone who can help you. There are a lot of people out there who feel the need to nurture an up-and-coming type like you. Unfortunately, their desire for a protege may not necessarily be proportional to their ability to help. So ask yourself: has that person accomplished what you want to accomplish? Do you respect him or her? Would you be proud to be associated with him or her?

When you find a potential mentor, don't be afraid to do a little courting. Let the person know you're available. Show your best side. Show that you can be the kind of protege he or she would respect and be proud to be associated with.

Be careful of initial infatuation. There seems to be a natural human inclination, when entering an emotional relationship of any kind, to work to ensure its permanence. Mentorship is no exception. Your mentor will probably give you too much, thus ensuring your indebtedness. Likewise, you will swear your undying allegiance to his or her projects, profession, philosophy and way of doing things. There is a tendency to overlook the faults of the other person...and to hide your own. But when these faults finally rear their ugly heads, and they always do, the entire relationship can be threatened. Try to keep a balanced perspective.

Also, as is typical of emotional relationships, the mentor relationship tends to end hard. But end it must, and the protege is usually the one to end it. There is only so much you can learn from a mentor, and you'll learn it fairly quickly if your relationship is a good one. Then it's time to move the relationship into a new phase of friendship based on equality and mutual respect—a relationship that can be maintained even if you someday surpass your mentor. That may all sound perfectly reasonable, but it's difficult to execute. Your mentor may react to your independence like a possessive parent, and feel betrayed or taken advantage of. And you may buy that, too, especially when you consider all the mentor has done for you and all the promises you made. You'd never think this could happen, but it does: the ideal relationship goes sour. And when it does, you could be left devastated. Sometimes there's just no easy way.

Mentors are not the only "helper" relationship you will have. You will almost certainly have *secondary mentors:* veteran professionals who give you assistance from time to time. And you will continue to have *role models* as you have all your life. Like Laurence Olivier is to an aspiring actor, a role model may be someone you have never met, but who has characteristics you admire and emulate.

The most important consideration in any of these relationships is keeping a critical eye out. Don't buy everything from anybody, and don't become a groupie of someone you admire. When you hold someone up to that kind of adulation it can actually hold you back, because you cannot allow yourself to surpass him or her. Some people, for instance, find it tough to imagine earning more money than their parents, reaching a higher position than their mentor, or receiving more recognition than a role model. It *can* happen, however, if you don't preclude it. Be selective, not only about the mentors and role models you choose, but also about the characteristics you choose to emulate.

Experts

As a professional in the Real World you will be surrounded by experts—people you count on to perform a certain service better than you can. Your accountant will be your expert in tax and money management, your secretary will be your expert in typing and filing. You may have to deal daily with computer experts, law experts, financial experts, science experts, communication experts and other experts. In fact, you will be some sort of expert yourself. Expertise is the very basis of teamwork.

When you deal with experts keep this in mind: being a professional requires that you continuously question and evaluate the data you have to process. You are the one responsible for your actions, and accountable for their consequences. Evaluating information is one of the few means of quality control. Therefore, working with experts does not mean you should trust everything they say. Experts may seem to be gurus, but they're not. They are fallible; sometimes they are flat-out wrong. It is just good business to ask for proof, even from a trusted expert. Professionalism demands that you hold out on a decision until you are sure, in *your* mind, a particular course of action is best.

Many experts will try to guard their expertise, and use it as a means of power. You can recognize these people in a minute. They complicate rather than simplify, obfuscate rather than clarify—all in an effort to create a mystique about their knowledge. Usually they have become accustomed to having their work accepted, and advice taken, without question. They will typically be aghast at your gall in questioning them. After all, it is they, not you, who are the experts in their fields.

Maybe so, but it is you, not they, who is the expert in your problem. *Never let anyone—no matter how expert—tell you what you want.* Even the most high-powered expertise can be evaluated in terms of common sense.* As a professional, you have the right and duty to evaluate it.

Seek out experts who are willing to form a partnership with you, who will try to make you knowledgeable about their field, and encourage you to show them how they can best help you. Acknowledge their authority without treating them as authority figures. A hidden advantage to this approach is that when you let experts know you will

---

*And it is the high-powered, complex variety that is usually most lacking in common sense.

not automatically defer to them, you get their best work.

While it's true that dealing with experts demands a certain degree of toughness, toughness is not to be confused with an attitude of distrust. The higher you get in the professional world, the more you must trust experts. The best posture is a general attitude of trust, but tempered with the understanding that no one knows everything about anything.

Your Mission Impossible Team

Although you probably won't be faced with it for a while, it's not too soon to start thinking about supervising other people. It's a big and important subject to any professional.

The many accepted (yet often conflicting) principles of leadership and people-management could fill a book—and many have (see our reading list for a few of the better ones)—so we won't even attempt to present an overview here.

However, we would like to share with you one analogy that Jimmy often promotes: the Mission Impossible Team. Your Mission Impossible Team is the core group of people you direct and depend on to produce the results you are paid to produce. Note that we said *core* group. Your Mission Impossible Team does not include the cast of everyone you supervise, but rather the handful of people you deal with closely and directly. If you are a manager, your Mission Impossible Team probably consists of your key staff members; if you are an entrepreneur, it consists of important suppliers; if you are an independent artist, it consists of your agent and benefactors.

The critical characteristic of any member of your team is that he or she can be counted on to perform "the impossible"...by working late, being creative, sticking his or her neck out, or whatever it takes to get the job done. To take the Mission Impossible analogy a step further, think of the team as your own personal cadre, trained to "assassinate" on command.

When you have team members with this kind of commitment, there is a temptation to make excessive or unreasonable demands. Don't do it. Remember, professional partnerships are 50-50. You have to give back as much as you take. The best way to give back to your Mission Impossible Team is to keep the team progressing. When your team members can see the advantages to being on your team, they will be more dedicated and motivated.

The fastest way to establish your own Mission Impossible Team is to earn a reputation as an out-standing member of another one. Be the most reliable, consistent performer you can be, and word will spread. Those who count on you will see that by providing you with the resources you need to build your own team they will be enabling you to deliver results on a greater scale. The process is natural: become an outstanding player and you'll soon be captain of your own team.*

Difficult Partners

They're everywhere, they're everywhere!

---

*Which does not imply that a person cannot be a captain of one team and member of another at the same time. Most professionals play both roles concurrently throughout their careers.

It's true. The professional world is full of difficult people: aggressive people, passive people, manipulative people, intimidating people, unreasonable people, insensitive people, selfish people and other assorted bad apples. You run into them on every level: bosses, co-workers, clients, subordinates, customers and suppliers. The business world seems to have a higher percentage of difficult people than the regular world has, probably because people feel freer to be difficult in a business context than they do in a personal context.

Which leads us to the first rule of dealing with difficult people: accept the fact that they exist. Don't waste energy resenting them. Get rid of the notion that you have to like everyone you do business with, or that everybody will necessarily approach a given situation the way you would. How much better than resisting and resenting difficult people it is to simply learn how to deal with them.

Of course, you do have to draw certain lines regarding the definition of "difficult." Nobody is expected to deal with someone who is abusive or hopelessly dishonest. And you may come to the conclusion that a difficult person is of such little value to you that he or she is simply not worth the trouble. Each of us has to define our own limits.

But keep in mind that even the most difficult people can be reasoned with on some level (they have to be or they wouldn't be in business). If you look at difficult people from this perspective, and learn how to handle them, you'll find that you are a much more successful, confident, and ultimately satisfied professional.

As an example of how to deal with one kind of

difficult person, Jeff relates: "I have a client who once backed out of a deal. We had spent an entire afternoon in my office negotiating a rather complex agreement on several months' worth of work: scheduling, prices, payment terms…the whole bit. But a few days later, when I went to his office to present some preliminary work and discuss more of the details, he denied ever having made the commitments he'd made. When I objected, he gave me a look of confusion and started explaining, 'But don't you remember when I said…and you said…and then we discussed…?' and proceeded to fabricate, in great detail and with wide-eyed sincerity, a conversation that had absolutely never taken place. I couldn't believe my ears—the guy was better than DeNiro. In fact, I think I was more fascinated by his performance than offended by his dishonesty.

"But what could I do? There was nothing to be gained by trying to reason with him point by point. That would have just turned into a 'No I didn't/Yes you did' volley.

"Of course, I could have become indignant and told him flat-out that he knew as well as I knew that he had made certain commitments, and further, he knew I knew he knew. But then where would I be? The guy still wanted to do business; he just wanted to do less of it and do it a little differently. I was suffering no real loss, since he was just backing out of future commitments. If he was actually cheating me on work I had performed, I would have burned the bridge without a second thought.

"I'm guessing he had just gotten caught up in the energy of the initial negotiation and, after thinking about it awhile, decided he had agreed to too much.

It's too bad he couldn't have just admitted that to me, and chose instead to lie his way out of it. But that's the way some people operate.

"So, rather than confront him, I simply said that I had a completely different recollection of the meeting and, obviously, there was a misunderstanding. From that moment on, I was clear that he was a person who could not be counted on to honor a 'gentleman's agreement.' And in the future every detail of every agreement we would ever make would have to be written down and signed by both of us before any work would commence. We've had a cooperative and productive working relationship ever since."

One of the best tricks for dealing with difficult people is to persist. When you have had conflicts with other people, it's natural to want to avoid them. In the professional world, however, that's rarely the best solution. It's better to grit your teeth, square your shoulders, and go right back. One of two things will happen:

1. They will be harder to deal with. In which case you may want to consider terminating the relationship. However, in certain cases you may decide that based on the overall productivity of the relationship, the difficulty is tolerable and worth enduring. Sometimes you can develop an implicit understanding with difficult people. You give them permission to be difficult—throw temper tantrums, for instance—while you both know that they are just fulfilling a need for catharsis. This may sound like a "sick" relationship, and in your personal life maybe it would be, but in the professional world it can be quite workable, provided the relationship is productive as a whole.

2. They will be easier to deal with. Difficult people know they are difficult. They're used to scaring people off, and they know when they run into a person who isn't so easily pushed around they've run into somebody special. In other words, you got their attention. You've shown that you value the relationship, and since you were the one to call after the conflict, you've demonstrated confidence and maturity. As a result, they may then allow you to enter their inner circle of professional partners who are not regular recipients of their unpleasantness.

The point is, difficult people *can* be dealt with. Sometimes it's even fun to figure out the best way to "handle" them. And occasionally you may have to leave your better instincts out of it.*

---

*A good reason not to be too self-righteous with difficult people is that maybe you were the one who was being difficult in the first place, and didn't realize it.

11: The Money Game*

Before we talk about how to play the money game, let's talk about why to play the money game.

If you're like most people, you'd like to have as much money as you can get. This is a natural attitude, and it is probably perfectly healthy and reasonable, provided it is kept in perspective.

The problem is it's tough to keep money in perspective. It's pretty powerful stuff. Many people fall in love with money. To them it is a source of excitement, an end in itself, the standard by which they judge the worth of things—and people. Others are totally turned off to money. They see it as a symbol of mankind's worst instincts, the "root of all evil."

In some ways both sides are right. To our society, money *is* a measure of the worth of things, including the worth of people. The more your talents are valued by society, the more society pays you for them. Money

---

*Any relationship between this chapter number and bankruptcy is purely coincidental.

is also power, in the sense that it enables you to do the things you want to do and make an impact on the things that matter to you.

On the other hand, money is rarely freedom. In fact, it is more often an enslaver—when it causes you to work at a job you hate, for instance, or to become obsessed with accumulating every possible penny.

That's why "the money game" is a good concept: it provides instant perspective. While one object of a game is to win, another is to enjoy yourself. And it's not the end of the world when you get a bad roll, make a bad move or even lose. For instance, think back to your twenty-year fantasy session. What were your goals? What experiences did you want to have? What kind of person did you want to become? Chances are you could achieve most of these with no more money than you have now.*

The biggest problem you are likely to have in playing the money game, as with any new game, is lack of confidence. Maybe you have never had much money, or it has been a long-time source of problems and anxiety. But as a professional you will probably earn a good amount of money (in case you haven't heard), and you owe it to yourself to take care of it. Start by getting used to it. And, most of all, relax. Money is like the opposite sex—once you get comfortable with it, you'll be surprised at how much fun it is to play with.

The following is an overview of the beginner's rules of the money game, as well as a couple of

---

*Unless your goal was—as it is for many people—to be rich. In that case our suggestion is to change your goal, because you will never be as rich as you want to be.

advanced plays. Consider them carefully. A sound money strategy can make a big difference in the quality of your life.

A Critical Distinction

The goal of most financial strategies is wealth, otherwise known as equity. To understand the concept of wealth, you must first understand another important financial concept, one with which you are probably more familiar: income. Income is the money you make, with gross income being the total amount, and net income being the amount after taxes. Net income is what we'll concentrate on here, because that is presumably all you have to work with.

Net income is the raw material of wealth. If you spend it, it's gone; if you save or invest it (successfully), it becomes wealth. Income is like winning a battle whereas wealth is like winning the war—because it is only after you have established a certain degree of wealth that your money can start providing to you its two best benefits: freedom and security.

Save, Save, Save

There's an old saying: "Spend $1 less than you make and your life will be a joy. Spend $1 more and it will be a struggle."

Obviously the $2 differential won't make much of a difference as far as what you can buy. But it makes all the difference in the world as to whether money is to ultimately be a positive or negative force in your life.

Sure, it's tough to save. Most of you reading this book have been students for the past few years, living on subsistence funds. We know what that's like. You barely have enough to pay your tuition and keep food and beer on the table, much less build a bankroll. Under these circumstances it is natural to get in the mind-set of spending every cent you can lay your hands on.

But your circumstances are soon to change. You are about to enter the Real World and finally start earning a real paycheck. It's an exciting transition. For some people it's a little too exciting. They go overboard and buy everything they ever wanted but couldn't afford, live over their heads and spend their way into serious debt. All because they didn't break the typical college mind-set of spending every cent (and then some).

You may think, "Not me." But don't be so sure. Getting a big jump in disposable income (such as when you go from being a student to getting a job) has been known to throw even the most level head off balance. Suddenly a whole new world of heretofore out-of-reach opportunities opens up. You see a million "ego goodies" (cars, clothes, stereos...) you think you can't live without. Furthermore, you can think of a million reasons why each is a smart investment: you need a new wardrobe to create the proper professional image ...a new car will save you on gas and repair bills...if you buy the expensive furniture you won't have to replace it so soon. Before you know it, you've made enough smart investments that you are in financial ruin.

We recommend a simple, one-stroke safeguard: put aside 10% of your paycheck (no matter how small it

is), and don't touch it—no matter what. Find a way
to maintain your lifestyle on 10% less than you make.
(It's amazing how many new graduates who made it
on $500 a month in college suddenly can't survive on
a nickel less than $1,500 a month!)

Saving money will enable you to start taking
advantage of the second greatest financial secret in
the world: interest. You've heard of it already? Maybe
so, but if you're like most college students you've
probably never had the opportunity to use it. In case
your memory needs refreshing, interest is the money
paid in return for depositing cash in a savings institution. The really neat thing about interest is that
it compounds itself. This means you earn interest on
your interest, so your savings grow at a faster rate.
In order to earn interest, though, you need what financial wizards refer to as liquid assets—in laymen's
terms, spare cash.

Before you can start really taking advantage of
interest opportunities, however, you should have at
least $1,000. This is generally the minimum needed
to qualify for a higher-than-average interest return.
*Never let your money sit in a commercial checking or
savings account earning 5¼%!* That may actually *cost*
you in real terms, because of inflation. But with at
least $1,000 you can buy stocks, bonds, money market
certificates and certificates of deposit—all of which
yield considerably higher returns than a conventional
savings account.

Many people are surprised that $1,000 is all that
is required to enter the world of "high finance." But
it's true. So make saving $1,000 a top priority.

Saving will become easier once you get in the
habit, particularly as you see your little stash turn-

ing into big bucks. The trick is don't get too involved with it in any way. Pretend it isn't even there. Don't even allow the issue to be raised as to whether or not it should be spent (become an automaton). If you find you have absolutely no self-discipline regarding your savings, look into a payroll savings plan whereby a fixed amount is automatically deducted from your check each pay period. That way you'll never even "see" what you're not missing.

These last points are important, because if you cannot make an emotional separation from your savings you'll never be able to bring yourself to take the best chance you've got of becoming rich.

The Best Chance You've Got of Becoming Rich*

Or, even more appealing: how to have all the money you'll ever need by age thirty.

We're not kidding. Depending upon your lifestyle objectives, it *is* possible to retire and live very comfortably by age thirty. All you'll need is $500,000 and a nice pastime to keep you occupied for the rest of your life. Follow our calculations and see how simple it is:

$500,000
X   12%   annual money market interest rate
$ 60,000   interest earned per year

At 12% annual interest rate (this is approximate; rates have fluctuated from 8% to 18% in the last few years) $500,000 invested in a money market certificate will earn $60,000 a year. The point is, you can live

---

*Short of marrying well.

like royalty on the interest alone, while you have 164 hours a week to work on what you *really* want to do.

The tough part, of course, is coming up with the half mil. That's a lot of money, and obviously you're never going to get it by age thirty saving your measly 10%.

Enter the *first* greatest secret in the world: leverage, an investment principle that makes compounded interest look like a night of penny-ante poker.

Leverage is a high-risk, high-gain financial strategy. It can make you very wealthy very quickly; it can also get you broke very quickly (even in the world of high finance you get nothing for nothing). Here are two oversimplified examples of how basic leverage can work.

1. Real estate leverage. Let's assume you buy a condominium for $40,000 (believe it or not, you still can in some places), put down 10% ($4,000) and mortgage (borrow) the balance ($36,000) at the current interest rate for thirty years. In five years you sell the place for the new market value of $65,000. After the realtor's commission and closing costs, you will have earned a clean $20,000 profit on your $4,000 cash investment, not to mention the equity you built and the taxes you saved (from deducting the interest from your taxable income) during your five years of ownership. That's a 500% rate of return! Incredible, huh? It happens all the time.

Real estate is generally considered to be among the safest investments. Land cannot be produced. There's a fixed supply of the stuff and the demand is always going up. Plus, you can buy at today's prices and pay with tomorrow's inflated dollars. (By the way, these are the exact numbers from Jimmy's first real estate transaction, so we know it works.)

2. Securities leverage. *Securities* is another word for stocks and bonds. Suppose that on the first of the month you bought 200 shares of an oil stock for $5.00 per share. That's a cash outlay of $1,000. By the end of the year the company hits five wells and the market value of the stock skyrockets to $10.00 per share. You then sell your shares at this price and make the fastest $1,000 you've ever seen. (200 x $10.00 = $2,000, less $1,000 cash outlay leaves a $1,000 profit. Deduct a small amount for the broker's commission, too.) That's a 100% return on your investment. Truly amazing, and again, it happens all the time. (The flip side of the coin, however, is that when it doesn't happen, you can end up a *big loser*. That also happens all the time.)

Now that you've got the idea, here's an example of how *super leverage* works. Let's say you bought 2,000 shares of that $5.00 per share oil stock on a "50% margin." This means you have to put down only 50% ($5,000), but you still own the entire 2,000 shares at the market value of $5.00 per share, or $10,000. Buying on margin, or "leveraging your position," is like a buy-now/pay-later deal whereby you always owe the other 50%, but you don't have to come up with it until later. In fact, you may never have to come up with it, provided the stock stays at the same price, or increases in value.

After one year, when the stock rises to $10.00 per share, you will have made $10,000 on your $5,000 investment—a 200% return! And that's enough to bring even Bunky Hunt to his knees. The down-side potential, however, is that if the stock drops to $2.50

per share, you would lose your $5,000 to cover what's referred to as a margin call, when you have to make up the negative difference on your position. Don't worry about technicalities; you can hire experts to take care of the details. Just make sure you understand the financial risk involved and are prepared to cover your losses.

Obviously, high-risk investment is not for the faint of heart. It is also not for the amateur. If you don't feel competent to handle your own investments (and if you're the slightest bit confused) go out and find yourself a good investment counselor. Check with several. Let each know precisely what your goals are (i.e., high risk / high return versus lower risk / lower return) and what your resources are, and see which one you feel most comfortable with.* As we said in the chapter on professional partners and experts, don't trust expertise blindly. You are the one ultimately responsible for your money, and even if you hook up with a responsible and competent counselor he or she will never care as much about your money as you do.

Also, never lose sight of the fact that even the best advice can be wrong. No matter how much experience and savvy you are able to recruit to back up your investment strategy, there will always be an element of gamble involved. So keep the central rule of gambling foremost in mind: don't bet the rent money.

Which brings us back to the 10% savings plan. Take some portion of this money (only as much as

*Ask your investment counselor to keep you posted on *all* your money options, from income averaging to tax strategies. You can speed your financial education by reading a good money overview book, such as *Where To Put Your Money* by N.Y. Times writer Peter Passell. It's the perfect book for new investors: easy to read and understand.

you'd be willing to lose) and earmark it as your investment "seed money." Then go out and take some chances with it! Remember, leverage is your single best shot of getting rich. The old "nest-egg" strategy of simply adding to your savings every two weeks will get you nowhere. Today, nobody gets rich by stuffing a mattress with dollars; they only get rich by putting them to work. And that 10% savings plan is the first critical step.

To sum it up:

1) Setting aside 10% of your income is not that tough, particularly if your income has just increased.*

2) If you lose part of it you won't miss it so much, because you never really "had" it.

3) If you invest your savings wisely, you'll be rich so fast you can forget about the Real World and go live on Fantasy Island.

Establishing and Maintaining Credit

One of the first things you should do after joining the Real World is obtain personal financial credit ...with banks, with utilities, with department stores, with the phone company, with credit agencies, with oil companies and with major credit card companies. Once you establish a track record as a sound, stable individual committed to repaying your debts in full and on time, you will be entitled to several short- and long-term privileges which our society bestows to make life easier and more convenient. Such as...

---

*10% is not a limit either. If you can live comfortably savings 15% or 20%, do it.

1. Instant credit. Most banks will grant credit-worthy customers a personal line of credit ($200 to $1,000-plus) from which the customer can draw whenever needed. For example, if you write a check for $500 and only have $200 in your account, the bank will advance you the additional $300 to cover the check. You can then pay it back on a monthly install-ment basis with interest, which is similar to how a revolving credit card payment plan works. A line of credit is convenient and will prevent you from ever bouncing a check by accident.

Also, it's a drag being caught without cash. If you have a personal line of credit, guaranteed check card or plastic money, you'll never have to worry about "stocking out" of money. And if you need an extra $50 after banking hours you can get it almost anywhere. With convenient, computerized tellers, you can con-vert credit-worthiness into cash at a moment's notice.

2. Credit cards. Once you get a department store card you can get an oil company card. Once you get those cards you can get a VISA card. Once you get a VISA card you can get a MasterCard. Then, you can parlay all that credit into the heavyweight, kingpin, total privilege plastic power symbol: the American Express Card. It's like a game. If VISA says you're good for it, so will MasterCard. And on and on. (There is a way to get an American Express card right out of college. We'll tell you how in a minute.)

3. More credit. By building your credit portfolio, you are also building your borrowing power. Once you take out a loan from any source and repay it, you'll be amazed to find how eager they are to lend you *more* money. In this way you can increase your credit limit from each source.

4. A house. As we all know, the American dream of owning a house is not coming true for everyone anymore.
But having established a sound credit record vis-a-vis
your credit card usage, not bouncing checks left and
right, and paying consistently on any car or durable
goods installment loans, you will have an easier time
securing major financing for a real estate purchase.
In this way, by establishing credit early, you are making a long-term investment in your future lifestyle.

How to Get Credit When You're Young

Let's take it from the beginning. Anyone who has
applied for credit and been turned down can tell you
how frustrating the process can be. In fact, there is
a built-in "Catch 22" in the credit approval system.
The number one reason most people are rejected on
loans and credit card applications is lack of a credit
history. When the approving officers have nothing to
go on to evaluate your credit-worthiness, they take the
safest course of action: they turn you down. Why
should they risk their necks?

The catch is obvious: how can you possibly establish a credit history if no one will grant you a line
of credit? You can't, unless you take some or all of the
following ten steps.

1. Get to know your banker. Go to see him or her twice
a year as you would your doctor and dentist. Even
though you may not start with a job paying six figures,
you should establish and maintain a rapport with your
banker. Let him or her know who you are, what you
do for a living, and what your career and financial

goals are. Prepare a personal financial statement*
showing your assets and liabilities, and provide your
bank with a copy. Update it each year, and then meet
with your banker to review any changes, as well as
the progress you've made toward your financial goals.

This will position you with a bank so that when
you apply for a loan of any sort, you'll be less of a
stranger. They'll know you, have your current statement on file, and — for those reasons alone—be more
inclined to lend you money. This will also save you
time, hassles and worry if you need money quickly.

2. Don't hop from bank to bank. Even if you move, don't
necessarily close one bank account and open another.
Hang in there with one bank and show some loyalty
and stability. Among loan officers it looks bad if you
have a history of constantly changing banks. You may
be viewed as an unprofitable account.

3. Keep a savings account during college. If you can
demonstrate your ability to save even a small amount
during those lean college years, you'll appear finan-
cially responsible and mature. Even loan officers
recognize what an achievement saving money in
college is.

4. Register with a credit bureau. Go to your local credit
bureau and request a printout of your credit record.

---

*As pretentious as it sounds, you really should prepare a finan-
cial statement as soon as you graduate. Even if you think you have
no equity, you may be surprised to find out how much you're really
worth. Between you car, clothes, savings (yes, even that $10 left in
your account after you drained it last time), insurance policy and
any inheritance you've received or have coming, it can add up. While
you're at it, you should also prepare a will and keep it on file with
your attorney.

(A credit bureau must, by law, give you a copy of your record if you request it. If they tell you that you don't have one, have them start one.) Then, go over each listing and piece of information with the clerk to ensure it's accurate and up-to-date. This is critical because lending institutions *always* request a copy of your credit record when evaluating whether to issue credit. And if your credit report is outdated and missing important information, you may be unfairly turned down.*

Jimmy learned this the hard way. After being rejected twice on his American Express application, he met with the local credit bureau and discovered his record was missing one key piece of information: he had applied for, and been issued, both a Master-Card and a VISA card two years before, and each showed good payment records. After updating his file and reapplying to American Express, his application was instantly approved and he was issued a card.

5. Get a guarantor. When applying for credit, have a family member, relative, or friend co-sign your application, so if you default (don't pay up) that person will be responsible. Most credit card companies and all banks are amenable to this method of lending money. It's done all the time because everyone wins in the transaction: a lending institution covers its bet (with the assets of your guarantor), you get credit, and your co-signer doesn't have to put up a dime (assum-

---

*An incorrect credit report can also cost you a job. Often prospective employers will request a credit report on you prior to making a job offer. They too want to make sure you're a responsible person.

ing, of course, you repay the debt). After borrowing money in this manner and successfully repaying it, you may not be required to produce a co-signer in the future. You'll have demonstrated credit-worthiness and a propensity to repay debts. This is a great way of establishing a sound credit record.*

6. Write a letter. Let's say you've been rejected twice on a credit card application for lack of credit history. Even though you feel you are a responsible person and have a sufficient income to qualify, you are continually turned down. Try writing a letter to whomever processed your application stating everything you can think of to change his or her mind. Let that person know all the mitigating factors in your lack of credit history. It is perfectly reasonable to admit that until recently you were being supported by your parents while attending college. It also looks good if you can add that you've just been hired for your first job.

In the letter explain why you want a credit card and what you plan to do with it (i.e., use it for convenience, business or travel). By taking the initiative and giving the credit-approving clerk more data to go on than the information on the standard application, you may be approved on your third try. It's worth the extra effort.

7. Apply before you graduate from school. As of this writing, American Express has a program stipulating

---

*We recommend you take out a small loan as soon as possible. Put the money in a savings account and repay the loan from the account. Doing so will cost you a few extra dollars in interest differential, but it's a small price to pay for establishing credit-worthiness at a young age.

if you are a graduating senior and have accepted future employment at an annual salary of $10,000 or more, they'll issue you a card now. This is the easiest way in the world to obtain an American Express card. You can find out about this program by looking on campus bulletin boards for their "take-one" coupon promotions, or by writing directly to American Express, P.O. Box 1885, New York, NY 10008...that's P.O. Box 1885, New York, NY 10008. We know this sounds like an ad, but it *is* the most important credit card you'll need. Take advantage of this special offer while you can. You'll be glad you did. (Okay, American Express, pay up).

8. Reapply. Sometimes all you have to do after credit rejection is reapply. Because of either a policy change, an increase in your salary, age, or length of employment, you may suddenly be deemed credit-worthy and issued a card.

9. Try your own bank first, then shop around. Whenever seeking a loan, a line of credit, or a major credit card, talk to your own bank first. Share your background information with your banker and ask for his or her help. If it's a loan you seek, you can demonstrate your credit-worthiness by pointing out your excellent history of making regular deposits and not bouncing checks. If it's a credit card you seek, you could have him or her write a letter of recommendation substantiating your outstanding credit record. Provided you've been a good, loyal customer, your own bank can help you as much or more than anyone else when seeking credit. But if they do turn you down, don't hesitate to try another source.

10. Don't be a deadbeat. Once you get credit, don't blow it by repeatedly missing payment deadlines and spending beyond your credit limit. Doing so will earn you the reputation of a deadbeat and hurt your chances of obtaining credit when you really need it. Every time you miss a payment date, it appears on your credit record as a demerit against you. Don't let an abused credit privilege hurt you later on.

12: The Brass Ring

Most books of this sort end with a pep talk, but this one will be an exception.

If you're like most recent graduates, you're coming off several long years of pep talks. You already know that the Real World awaits you, that it is a challenge, and that you are responsible for your own success. You already know you have to give it everything you've got, set your sights high and never give up. You already know, to use a fine old cliche from your days on the merry-go-round, that now is the time to "grab for the brass ring."

This is all good advice, but only to a point. Enthusiasm and ambition without a sense of direction will get you nowhere—or worse, somewhere you don't want to be. Pep is something that should always be kept in perspective.

Focusing your professional energies and maintaining a sense of direction requires deliberate effort. It requires that you periodically reexamine your goals and assumptions, and make any necessary adjustments in your course. Here is a simple, effective technique for achieving this: any time you find yourself gearing up to grab for another brass ring, whatever it may be, step back for a moment and ask yourself the following three questions.

1. "Do I Really Want It?"

The blunt fact is that most people conduct their careers according to other people's expectations. They dutifully enter the career they were groomed for by their parents and teachers. On the job they do everything they feel is implicitly or explicitly expected of them, but nothing more. For them, work could never be a means of expression or fulfillment—or anything more than a means to money and status.

That's no way to live. Nor is it a way to succeed. To muster the energy and enthusiasm it takes to really make it in the professional world—and it takes a lot—you must love what you do. Otherwise it is too much hard work. And in the final analysis it is inspiration, not hard work, that breeds success.

It is important to keep your career moving in the direction of your greatest enjoyment and satisfaction. Put simply, you must identify the aspects of your job that you like, and then expand them. Direct your energy toward that which gives you the biggest thrill. At the same time, let go of the boring or anxiety-producing aspects. The key is to make this an ongoing, everyday process.

Fortunately, professionals today are more and more free to engineer their own careers. Organizations are reaching new levels of flexibility and individual accommodation. Job descriptions are becoming obsolete—no two functions need be alike.

Your pursuit of professional happiness may lead you to places you never expected to go (you may find that the voice telling you to join the merchant marines was the one you should have listened to all along). But be open to it. You'll never regret it.

As actor Michael Moriarty said, "Why achieve mere excellence when you can achieve happiness?"

2. "Why Do I Want It?"

As yoga master Sri Swami Sachidananda told a gathering of the faithful in Boulder a couple of years ago, "Want nothing and you will have everything." He explained, "If you want something, all you will end up with is something. If you want nothing, you will end up with everything. Nothing and everything look alike."

Swami, himself a great achiever, was probably overstating his case a bit. But he was not talking nonsense. On the contrary, for those of us writing books of advice (and reading books of advice), Swami's is some of the best advice around.

"No way," you say. "There are ten thousand things I want. Furthermore, I want to continue to want them, and someday to have them."

Therein lies the rub. When do we ever "have" what we want? So often we dedicate ourselves to the pursuit of a goal thinking that once we achieve it we will have it made. We deny ourselves, put everything else on hold, and set out on a single-minded quest for achievement. We think, "If I work hard and sacrifice now, later things will be rosy."

But with that kind of attitude things will never be rosy. How many times have you achieved a major goal (getting into a certain college, entering a relationship, buying a new toy) only to find out that it wasn't quite what you expected and didn't necessarily make you any happier?

The process of living for anticipated fulfillment can go on indefinitely, with the ante always being upped, and fulfillment always just out of reach. It's an easy trap to fall into, one your authors know about firsthand. As Jimmy says of his Mercedes 380SL, "The most fun I had with it was the day before I picked it up."

The point is, while you're grabbing the brass ring, don't forget to enjoy the ride.

3. "Is It Worth Wanting?"

One of the goals of our generation, it seems, is to get rid of guilt. Maybe we do have too much unwarranted guilt in our lives. But that doesn't mean it is necessarily wrong to feel guilt. Guilt is a natural feeling. Like pain it alerts us that something is wrong. There are many things we all do, and many conditions we all tolerate that are eminently worthy of our guilt. For example, during the sixty seconds last Saturday night that you and your date spent discussing the relative merits of sauce Bearnaise versus sauce Bordelaise over Chateaubriand, 114 people died of hunger.

Ah ha! You think you've spotted an inconsistency in our message. It is true that a major thesis of this book is that a realistic view of life must recognize its inherent inequalities, that wealth is not immoral, and that people should enjoy not only their labor but also the fruits of it (we both happen to prefer Bearnaise).

But isn't it also true that we who have been lucky enough to have our minds stimulated, skills developed, bodies fed and egos stroked should feel some responsibility to direct our resulting intelligence, expertise and power toward helping those who have not been so charmed?

We think so. But considering the magnitude and stubbornness of the world's problems, what can we do, realistically, to make a difference? Give a few bucks to Jerry's Kids? Visit our senile grandmother in the nursing home? Challenge a drunk who bad-mouths the boat-people? Write our congressperson?

Yes—all of these—and anything else that feels right.

No contribution is too small. Giving back to society is not an event. It is a frame of mind that recognizes that our responsibilities extend further than to just ourselves.

These responsibilities are particularly important to us as professionals, and they should be factors in every action we take.

On Second Thought...

Forget what we said a minute ago about not ending this book with a pep talk. We didn't realize how hard it would be to resist (just wait till you write a book).

Here it is.

You are a member of the most sophisticated and educated generation in history, with an array of options that would have been inconceivable even a few years ago. The Real World is an exciting place, it's scary, it's a challenge, and it demands nothing less than your best. But it's worth it.

So go out there, figure out what you want, choose your partners, know which way the wind's blowing, play well the games you choose, make a contribution, and enjoy yourself.

That's pretty much all there is to it.

Further Reading

Arnold, John D. *Make Up Your Mind!* (New York: Amacom, 1978.)
How to make the "right decision."

Bates, Jefferson D. *Writing With Precision.* (Washington, D.C. Acropolis Books Ltd., 1980.)
A practical approach to writing simply and clearly.

Bolles, Richard Nelson. *What Color Is Your Parachute?* (Berkeley, Calif.: Ten Speed Press, 1972.)
The classic "career changer" book.

Bolles, Richard Nelson. *The Three Boxes of Life.* (Berkeley, Calif.: Ten Speed Press, 1978.)
If your life seems to be at a standstill, read this book.

Bromberg, Murray and Melvin Gordon. *1100 Words You Need To Know.* (New York: Barron's Education Series, 1971.)
A vocabulary book that actually works.

Campbell, David. *If I'm in charge here why is everybody laughing?* (Allen, Texas: Argus Communications, 1980.)
Full of useful tips for managers and supervisors.

Campbell, David. *If you don't know where you're going, you'll probably end up somewhere else.* (Allen, Texas: Argus Communications, 1974.)
Goal-setting at its best.

Campbell, David. *Take the road to creativity and get off your dead end.* (Allen, Texas: Argus Communications, 1977.)
A lively exploration of creativity.

Coulson, Robert. *The Termination Handbook.* (New York: The Free Press, 1981.)
A book for those on both sides of the "firing lines."

Davies, Don and Bern Wheeler. *Standing Ovation or Polite Applause?* (Ontario, Canada: St. George Press, 1981.)
Short, pithy book on how to prepare and deliver formal speeches.

Drucker, Peter F. *Management: Tasks, Responsibilities, Objectives.* (New York: Harper & Row, 1980.)
Concerns the immediate future of business.

Drucker, Peter F. *Managing in Turbulent Times.* (New York: Harper & Row, 1980.)
A new classic on how to do business in today's professional world.

Fuller, R. Buckminster. *Critical Path.* (New York: St. Martin's Press, 1981.)
An entire lifetime of thought and concern by "the planet's friendly genius."

Glasser, William. *Positive Addiction.* (New York: Harper & Row, 1976.)
How to get hooked on things that are good for you.

Hampton, David, Charles E. Summer and Ross A. Webber. *Organizational Behavior and the Practice of Management.* (Glenview, Ill.: Scott, Foresman & Company, 1968.)
Jimmy's most memorable college textbook (probably the only one he ever read). We had to have one in there.

Herbert, Frank. *Without Me You're Nothing.* (New York: Simon and Schuster, 1980.)
Demystification of computer by the author of *Dune*.

Korda, Michael. *Success!* (New York: Random House, Inc., 1977.)
Fun reading, but don't take Korda too seriously.

LaBella, Arleen and Dolores Leach. *Personal Power.* (Boulder, Colorado: New View Press, 1983.)
Straight talk for today's working woman.

Lewis, Norman. *How To Read Better & Faster.* (New York: T.Y. Crowell, 1978.)
A do-it-yourself lesson on speed reading, for those who can do it without Evelyn Woods.

Mackenszie, R. Alec. *The Time Trap.* (New York: McGraw-Hill, 1972.)
How to get more done in less time.

Mancuso, Joseph. *Fun & Guts.* (Rowley, Mass.: The Entrepreneurs Club, Unltd., 1973.)
Must reading for those who plan on trying "the hustle." Just as good as Townsend's classic *Up the Organization*.

Nierenberg, Gerard I. *The Art of Negotiating.* (New York: Hawthorn Books, 1968.)
The first book ever written on the subject...and the best.

Pascarella, Perry. *Industry Week's Guide To Tomorrow's Executive.* (New York: Van Nostrand Reinhold Company, 1981.)
A humanistic approach to management in the corporation of the future.

Pettus, Theodore. *One on One.* (New York: Random House, 1981.)
How to handle the job interview...where it all counts.

Ries, Al and Jack Trout. *Positioning: The Battle for Your Mind.* (New York: McGraw-Hill, 1980.)
How to communicate in an over-communicated society. A must for marketing majors.

Ruben, Harvey L. *Competing.* (New York: Lippincott & Crowell, 1980.)
How our drive to achieve can be applied in healthy and positive ways.

Rutherford, Robert. *Just In Time.* (New York: John Wiley & Sons, Inc., 1981.)
Help for the time-pressured. Packed with anecdotes.

Sarnoff, Dorothy. *Make the Most of Your Best.* (Garden City, N.Y.: Doubleday & Company, Inc., 1970.)
How to present yourself and your ideas with confidence.

Schwimmer, Lawrence D. *How To Ask For a Raise Without Getting Fired.* (San Francisco: Harper & Row, 1980.)
Assertiveness on the job: how you can increase self-assurance, promotability and effectiveness.

Stein, Ben. *Moneypower.* (New York: Harper & Row, 1979.)
How to put the forces of inflation to work for your money.

Strunk, William, Jr., and E.B. White. *The Elements of Style.* (New York: MacMillan Publishing Co., Inc., 1972.)
The all-time classic on the fundamentals of writing. Read it.

Sugarman, Joseph. *Success Forces.* (Chicago: Contemporary Books, 1980.)
Six truths about success written by a mail-order maverick.

Toffler, Alvin. *The Third Wave.* (New York: William Morrow and Company, Inc., 1980.)
If you read only one book about the future, let this be the one.

Townsend, Robert. *Up The Organization.* (New York: Alfred Knopf, 1978.)
Hilarious book on modern business written by the man who turned Avis around ("We try harder," remember?). Believe 85% of it.

Walker, Glen. *Credit Where Credit Is Due.* (New York: Rinehard and Winston, 1979.)
Everything you ever wanted to know about credit.

Zinsser, William. *On Writing Well.* (New York: Harper & Row, 1980.)
One of the few books on the subject that's actually fun to read. Just reading it will improve your writing automatically.

IN SEARCH OF EXCELLENCE
Thomas J. Peters and   *(K37-844, $8.95, U.S.A.)*
Robert H. Waterman, Jr.   *(K37-845, $10.75, Canada)*
Highly acclaimed and highly optimistic about the future of American management, this essential book proves that American business is alive and well—and successful! Subtitled "Lessons from America's Best-Run Companies," it reveals the secrets of the art of successful American management, the eight fascinating basic principles that the authors found hard at work at Johnson & Johnson, Procter & Gamble, IBM, Hewlett-Packard, Delta Airlines, McDonald's, and other well-run firms. Here are the native American policies and attitudes that lead to growth and profits—policies and attitudes that thousands of business people all over the country are now trying for themselves!

MEGATRENDS
Ten New Directions Transforming Our Lives
John Naisbitt
    Hardcover: (K51-251, $17.50, in U.S.A.; $20.00 in Canada)
    Paperback: (K90-991, $3.95 in U.S.A.; K32-035,
    $4.95 in Canada)
Once in a great while a book so accurately captures the essence of its time that it becomes the spokesman for that decade. In 1956 it was *The Organization Man.* In 1970 it was *Future Shock.* In the 1980's it will be *Megatrends,* the only "future" book whose predictions for tomorrow are based on a dynamic analysis of what America is today. As Naisbitt details America's shift from industrial production to providing services and information, you can project your career and business moves. As you learn where the new centers of activity are developing, you can decide where you should live. If you have political goals, John Naisbitt's analysis of governmental trends can help you target your energies. This is the challenge, the means, and the method to better our lives . . . a must for everyone who cares about the future.

Look for this—and other Warner bestsellers—in your bookstore. If you can't find them, you may order directly from us by sending your check or money order for the retail price of the book, plus 75¢ per order and 50¢ per copy to cover postage and handling, to: WARNER BOOKS, P.O. Box 690, New York, NY 10019. New York State and California residents must add applicable sales tax. Please allow 4 weeks for delivery of your books.